CHILDREN OF THE SIEGE

Pauline Cutting attended Liverpool University and worked in Liverpool before she achieved first her F.R.C.S. then a locum consultancy at the Medway Hospital in Gillingham at the early age of thirty-two. She worked at Queen Mary's Hospital, Roehampton before answering an advertisement in a medical journal asking for volunteers to work in the Palestinian refugee camps in Beirut. She continues to work for Medical Aid for Palestinians, the British charity that sent her to Beirut.

In July 1987 Dr Cutting was awarded an OBE for her work in Beirut.

CHILDREN OF THE SIEGE

Pauline Cutting

Pan Books
in association with William Heinemann

First published in hardback 1988 by William Heinemann Ltd
and simultaneously in paperback by Pan Books Ltd,
Cavaye Place, London SW10 9PG
in association with William Heinemann Ltd
9 8 7 6 5 4 3 2 1

Printed in Great Britain by
Richard Clay Ltd, Bungay, Suffolk

To Ben, my family and all the
people of Bourj al Barajneh camp

Contents

Illustrations

Photographs are reproduced by kind permission of the following: nos. 1, 5, 9, 10, 11 and 12, Times Newspapers Ltd; nos. 2, 3, 4, 6, 8, 13 and 14, Ben Alofs; no. 15, Popperfoto; nos. 16 and 17, Topham.

Acknowledgements

I should like to thank Dr Rede, Director of Haifa Hospital, for his unswerving support, and all my other colleagues in the PRCS at the hospital. I should also like to thank all at Medical Aid for Palestinians whose dedication and hard work have provided inestimable aid in the Lebanon and finally got us home safely. I also owe a great debt to the journalists who exposed the plight of Bourj al Barajneh to the world, especially Brent Sadler and his Lebanese colleague, Marie Colvin, Tom Stoddart and Nura Bustani, who all risked their lives coming into the camp.

I shall never be able adequately to express my gratitude to my family, who endured the nightmare with extraordinary courage and patience, often in front of the television cameras.

Mary Jones typed the manuscript with remarkable speed and accuracy, having to decipher my illegible doctor's scribble. Lisa Glass and Hugo de Klee at Heinemann both worked on the manuscript under great pressure.

I should like to thank my editor, Dan Franklin, and my agent, Xandra Hardie for reading, criticising and constantly encouraging the writing.

Finally, I must say thank you to all the other foreign health workers who shared with me most of the experiences described in this book – Ben, Susie, Sol-Britt, Lieve, Dirk, Hannes, Barbara, Swee, Alberto and Chris Giannou.

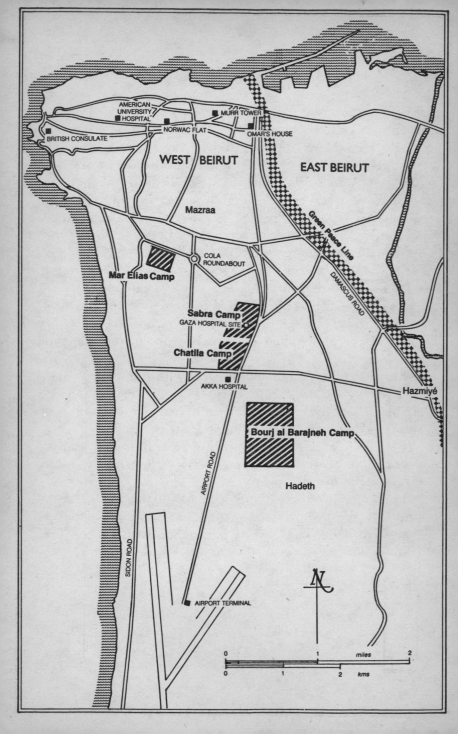

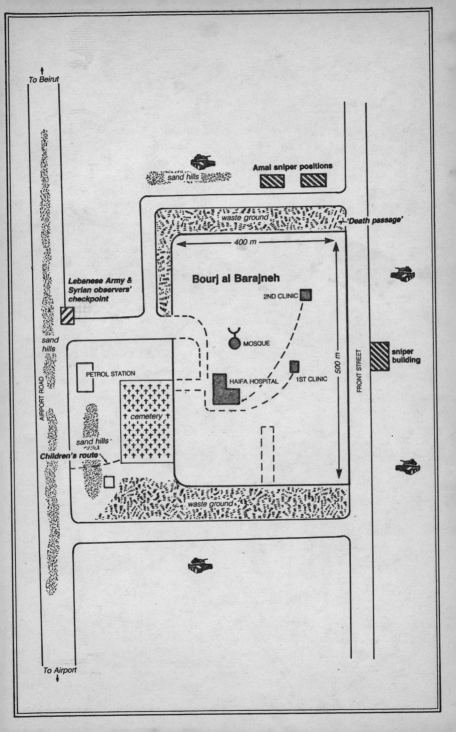

Author's Note

Most of the people described in this book are still in Beirut. In a number of cases I have changed their names in order to protect their lives.

P.C.

Prologue

On the last day of December 1986 a small boy called Bilal was crossing an alley in the Palestinian refugee camp of Bourj al Barajneh in southern Beirut. High in a building outside the camp a sniper belonging to the Amal militia was watching that alleyway. When Bilal came into his sights he squeezed the trigger.

Bourj al Barajneh had been under siege for two months and Bilal was one of the hundreds of its inhabitants who had become casualties of that small, bloody war that was being waged in a corner of Beirut, unnoticed by the rest of the world.

I was in the emergency room of Haifa Hospital in the centre of the camp when Bilal was brought in on a stretcher. The bullet had passed through his right arm, both sides of the back of his chest and out through his other arm. My first sight of that child I will carry in my mind until the day I die. He was a beautiful dark curly-haired boy of seven years, with a cherubic face and dark brown eyes. Both his arms and both sides of his chest were bleeding through his T-shirt. He was not crying or struggling, but his lips were blue and he was gulping for air like a fish out of water. The stretcher-bearers put him down on the couch and Mashour, a nurse, cut off his clothes. Dr Samer at once put a drip in his foot. I gave him an injection of local anaesthetic, then inserted a chest drain tube into one side of his chest. Dr Samer did the same for the other side of his chest. As the blood drained out from his chest and his lungs re-expanded, the blue turned back to pink and he was not quite so hungry for air. We gave him a blood transfusion to replace the lost blood and took him to X-ray.

By this time I was aware that Bilal had not moved his legs once since he had arrived at the hospital. I promptly did some tests, pinching his legs. It became clear that he could not feel either of them. The bullet had cut his spinal cord. He would be paralysed from the waist down for the rest of his life.

I had been working in Bourj al Barajneh for 13 months by then, and I had seen many injured children. But for some reason Bilal's case moved me like none of the others. What had this little boy done to deserve such a fate? What part had he played in the struggle that was raging around me?

He had done nothing, of course, and he had played no part. He was just a small boy who had been in the wrong place at the wrong time. A small Palestinian boy.

I thanked God that the injuries to Bilal's arms were only flesh wounds. He was going to need his arms to move around in the future.

We put him in a bed on the ground floor of the hospital, then tipped it up slightly to help drain his chest.

He smiled.

Chapter 1

As the aeroplane approached Beirut International airport on 6 December 1985, I was nervous. I was coming to Lebanon to work as a surgeon and, although I had been fully briefed in London, I was not sure what to expect.

Seen from the air at a distance, Lebanon has a timeless, striking beauty and my first impressions of Beirut remain, even now, some of the most vivid. Snow-capped mountain peaks of the Mount Lebanon range run parallel with the coast only a few kilometres inland and the white city of Beirut stands prominently on the rocky headland of Ras Beirut. But, as the plane came in to land, the beauty faded and my anxiety returned. The scars of 10 years of civil war were all too apparent on the face of the once beautiful city. All around the airport stood buildings half destroyed by bombing.

As we left the plane and walked across the tarmac, we passed several groups of heavily armed men in military fatigues waiting around in the sunshine. Once through passport control, there were even more of them. I stifled my nervousness and strode on up the ramp on the other side, past more gun-carrying militiamen and along to the barriers where a hundred or so people were waiting for the arriving passengers. I was expecting to be met by Sol-Britt, the Norwegian Aid Committee co-ordinator in Beirut. There was only one tall, blonde woman, so it was not difficult to identify her. She seemed calm, kind and relaxed, an impression of Sol-Britt which was never to change, and I immediately felt better.

My journey to the Lebanon had begun one summer evening

3

earlier that year. I was sitting in my flat flicking through the job advertisements in the *British Medical Journal*. At the end of September I would be reaching the end of my current appointment as a junior hospital doctor in the burns and plastic surgery department at Queen Mary's Hospital, Roehampton. I had been thinking about going to work abroad as I was interested in seeing how other countries' health services operated, so I turned to the section advertising posts overseas.

One particular advertisement caught my eye. A British charity called MAP (Medical Aid for Palestinians) was seeking volunteers to work in the Lebanon.

'That looks interesting,' I thought.

As a qualified surgeon making a career in accident and emergency work, and with an interest in trauma and experience in burns and plastic surgery (more the reconstructive kind than the cosmetic), I thought my skills might be useful and that the work could be very challenging. I sent off my *curriculum vitae* and a letter of enquiry. Two days later, at work, I received a phone call from the secretary of MAP.

'I phoned,' she said, 'because there is a reception tomorrow night for Dr Swee Chai Ang and a team who have just returned from Lebanon. Please come if you can.'

At the reception at the MAP office in London Dr Swee Chai Ang, a tiny Malaysian orthopaedic surgeon, stood on a chair and spoke passionately to an audience of 40, mainly journalists and charity workers, about her six-week visit to Palestinian refugee camps in the Lebanon. She had gone there in June, just after an attack on the camps.

'During the first attack on the camps of Chatila and Bourj al Barajneh,' she told us, 'the wounded were not allowed out of the camps to hospitals. Many died as a result.'

I was shocked, feeling – as I think most doctors would – that for patients to die because they are deliberately denied access to hospital care is unacceptable.

Swee Chai Ang spoke about the continuing desperate lack of medical services and personnel, and the hundreds of people in the camps still needing surgery.

Impressed by Swee Chai Ang's compassion and drive, I sought her out among the throng and told her I was considering volunteering. She asked me about my work and experience in surgery. She also asked me how much I knew about the Lebanon and Palestinians.

'Not much,' I had to admit. 'Only what I've read in the papers and a little from two friends, a doctor and a nurse, who worked in Beirut during the Israeli invasion in 1982.'

'That's all right,' she said. 'I didn't know anything before I first went.'

The secretary, Ros, gave me two books to read, one, *Lebanon: The Fractured Country* by David Gilmour, and the other, *Palestinians, from Peasants to Revolutionaries* by Rosemary Sayigh.

A week later, having read sketchily through both books, I returned for a personal interview. Actually the interview was not very formal, more a discussion over coffee. Dr Rafiq Husseini, the chairman of MAP, and Ros, told me that MAP had been founded in 1984. They also revealed more about the work of their volunteers, about the Palestine Red Crescent Society, the Palestinian equivalent of the Red Cross, and about life in the Lebanon and the Palestinian refugee camps. They described the primitive living conditions in the camps but said that it was both safer and created more trust if the volunteers were prepared to live at least some of each week in the camp where they were working. They stressed that there was essentially no night-life in the camps and that it was better not to move around in the city after dark when the paramilitary militias took control of the streets.

It seemed they were deliberately painting a picture of a life that would be at best uncomfortable, at worst plain dangerous.

It didn't put me off. The more I heard, the more interested I became.

They suggested that I could go in October or November. Most MAP volunteers were engaged for only three months, so that if they could not bear the life it would not be too long away, and so that when they returned they could give MAP up-to-date information on the situation and the medical needs of the camps' inhabitants.

In November 1985 I attended a final two-day briefing session in which I saw videos about the Lebanon, explaining the geography and territorial disputes within the country. I was asked to sign a document saying that I would treat everyone regardless of race, religion or creed. This was a fundamental requirement of MAP and those volunteers not prepared to make such a commitment were not considered suitable. At the end of all the briefings I knew much more about what I was taking on but still did not really know what to expect. 'At least,' I thought, 'I'm better prepared to face the unexpected.'

Now that I was actually in the Lebanon I realised that no briefing, however thorough, can prepare one for the reality of Beirut. So volatile was the situation in the city that my arrival had been delayed for nearly three weeks by the closure of Beirut airport while a battle was fought between the two major militias of West Beirut, Walid Jumblatt's Progressive Socialist Party and Nabih Berri's Amal militia. The battle, known as the 'Flag War', had flared up after a dispute about the hanging of a flag, and had rapidly escalated into six days of fierce, full-blown street-fighting that had left dozens dead and hundreds wounded.

As Sol-Britt drove us in the small white ambulance towards the city, she pointed out the PSP and Amal militias still glaring at each other across road junctions. They were heavily armed with rocket launchers, even tanks, and the atmosphere still seemed very tense.

Sol-Britt told me that during the Flag War she had taken refuge in the southern part of West Beirut where there was no fighting. When she returned to the NORWAC flat in West Beirut after the fighting, she found that a bullet had shattered the window, passed through a cupboard and made holes in her underwear. She laughed at the look of alarm on my face. Sol-Britt herself seemed totally unafraid, and it was comforting to know that this capable Norwegian would be here to help and advise me.

Turning off the airport road we drove along a tarmac road for about 60 metres, then swung right towards the entrance to Bourj al Barajneh camp, where we were due to meet Barbara Bowman, a British nurse already working for MAP. As we bounced along on the unmade-up road inside the camp we passed a small car mechanics' workshop, a hairdresser's, a clothes shop and, on the right, a large, two-storey bomb-damaged building.

'What's that?' I asked.

'That is what remains of the Samed factory,' answered Sol-Britt. 'Before 1982 it was a fully functioning factory of several small workshops making furniture, bread, clothes and halva. Only the halva-making part is still working.'

After a further 50 metres the dirt road ended abruptly in front of a five-storey building. Above the double doorway was a sign saying PALESTINE RED CRESCENT SOCIETY. HAIFA HOSPITAL. CENTRE FOR EMERGENCIES. I glanced into the muddy entrance hall of the hospital, then followed Sol-Britt down a path beside it. At once, we entered a maze of narrow winding alleys. My first reaction was shock at the poverty and squalor. All the houses seemed overcrowded, full of people living on top of each other. The alleyways were thronged with children playing amongst open drains and water-pipes. The buildings of the camp had been damaged in the first rounds of the 'Camp War' and most of the breeze-block and plaster houses were pock-marked with bullet holes.

7

Barbara met us at the door of the NORWAC clinic where she lived and worked and at once offered us tea. A large woman in her early thirties from the north of England, she had previously worked in the outback of Australia, and had been in Bourj al Barajneh for four months. Her manner was very direct and friendly and she laughed a lot – loudly. Apparently, she had been told it was not the done thing for women to laugh loudly in the street, especially at night, and Barbara was trying to learn the Arabic for 'I'm sorry I laugh too much'. However, the children did not mind. They loved her and, as she walked back up through the camp with us, they ran after her, clamouring in English, 'Barbara, hello Barbara!', and to us the phrase that all the children use to strangers, 'What's your name? What's your name?'

After leaving the camp we drove for a mile along the airport road towards the city, then turned off and into the car-park of Akka Hospital. This was a Palestine Red Crescent Society hospital situated just across the road from Chatila camp.

'Most of the patients here are local Lebanese which is probably why it has survived,' Sol-Britt explained as we walked up to an office on the first floor. We were met by a smart, elegant woman in her late forties with black curled hair. This was Um Walid, head of the PRCS in Lebanon. She shook my hand warmly.

'Welcome,' she said. 'Do sit down and have some tea. You are the British surgeon aren't you?'

'Yes,' I replied.

'Good,' she said. 'Tomorrow you will go to Haifa Hospital and be in charge of the surgery department.'

I smiled bravely, but inwardly I was horrified. 'I've only been in the country an hour,' I thought, 'and already she wants to put me in charge of a surgery department!' I had been in charge of an accident and emergency department in England but never a surgery department, and until I had my feet on the ground I did not want to be in charge of anything.

Sol-Britt came to my rescue.

'Doctor Cutting has never been here before,' she explained, 'so I arranged for her to spend the first week in Chatila working with Dr Giannou. I think it would be better like that.'

Um Walid reluctantly agreed and I breathed a sigh of relief.

Driving into West Beirut after leaving Akka Hospital, I saw the destructive effects of the civil war close up. All the buildings bore the scares of shells and bullets, the sports stadium looked like a ruined amphitheatre from Ancient Greece. Some blocks of flats hit by shells on one side had their floors and stairways hanging in cascades down to the ground, while people still lived precariously in the other side. Here in West Beirut, the authority of the state was reduced to almost nothing. All the power was concentrated on the streets with the militias. The lack of any proper authority was immediately evident in the traffic. There were no road signs and no rules. Cars and trucks drove where they pleased, flashing their hazard-warning lights and headlights (if they still had them) to announce, 'I am going fast.' Many of the cars bouncing in and out of shell-holes were wrecks. No MOT here; cars were driven until they fell to pieces and many, including the NORWAC ambulance, had the already all-too-familiar bullet holes. When I asked Sol-Britt about the ones in the side of the ambulance, she laughed and assured me that most had appeared when the ambulance was not in use. 'In Beirut,' she said, 'even a dispute over a parking place can be settled with a gun.'

At the small NORWAC flat I had a quick and welcome shower. Then we set off for Chatila camp. Chatila was even more squalid than Bourj al Barajneh. It was much smaller, only 200 metres square, housing about 5,000 people, although there had once been 9,000. Many of the paths and alleys were not paved and as it had been raining intermittently for two months, the ways were muddy, with puddles everywhere. The winter weather in Beirut is like a British November stretched over five months: damp, cold and wet. Temperatures fall to near freezing. As in Bourj al Barajneh, there were open drains in the streets, overflowing after the rain, and garbage was piled up on plots of waste ground between the buildings, waiting for collection by the United Nations Relief and Works Agency (UNRWA), the organisation that was supposed to care for the needs of the Palestinian refugees. Again, there were damaged buildings everywhere, and curious children asking, 'What's your name?'

Sol-Britt led me to the centre of the camp on foot, to a small two-storey building with a red crescent above the door. There I was introduced to the doctor in charge of the camp hospital, Dr Chris Giannou. A Canadian surgeon of Greek/Macedonian origin, he was a small, wiry man with a penetrating gaze and an enormous Zapata moustache. Chris Giannou had been in Chatila for 10 weeks, building, organising and directing a sort of field hospital in a cluster of small houses in the centre of the camp. He had set up a newly equipped operating-theatre in a tiny room underground and miniature versions of the other departments associated with hospitals – three small 4-bedded wards, a pharmacy, an out-patient clinic, an X-ray room, all in different buildings. The rooms contained only the most basic equipment and as Dr Giannou proudly showed us around in his wellingtons, I saw already that this was a world away from the sophisticated hospital service of the British National Health Service that I was used to. At the end of the tour, Sol-Britt left and I was shown up to the staff quarters above the out-patient department. These, too, were very Spartan – two unheated rooms with 3 or 4 camp-beds and one cupboard in each, a minute kitchen and a bathroom with a hole-in-the-floor toilet, a sink and a shower, but no hot water.

As I dumped my bags on one of the beds and sat down, two Belgian doctors, Dr Lieve Seuntjens and Dr Dirk van Duppen, came in. They had been in Beirut for seven weeks and were organising a primary health care clinic in Chatila with plans to do the same thing in Bourj al Barajneh. They provided vaccinations and mother-and-child care, and advised on matters of hygiene (like sewage and clean water) and preventive medicine.

Seeing the look on my face, Lieve said, 'Don't worry, for the first month it's miserable, but after that you will actually enjoy living in the camps.'

Lieve was short, blonde and talkative. Dirk was tall and quietly spoken, with glasses. They were both in their late twenties and had been married for a few months. I liked them at once.

Two Palestinian nurses who lived in, so as to be on call, came upstairs with some Arab mint tea which they served in little clear glasses. As soon as I had finished my glass, they bombarded me with questions. What was my name? Was I married? How old was I? How many brothers and sisters did I have? I gathered that to be still unmarried at 33 and with only one brother and one sister I was a hopeless case. Eventually everyone left and, after wearily making a few notes in my diary, I fell asleep at midnight to the sound of distant gunfire. My first day in Beirut was over.

The next morning, after a freezing wash, I went to look for Chris Giannou to ask about my duties. I found him still in his pyjamas in the hospital foodstore, smoking a Gitane and talking heatedly in Arabic to several other men. The foodstore was apparently his temporary bedroom, the hospital meeting room and the staff dining-room. Before I could open my mouth, a rumbling noise started a few metres away, soon rising to a dreadful banging and crashing. 'What was that? Was it a bomb?' I asked nervously. All the old men laughed as Chris explained, 'It is only the hospital generator switching on.'

Breakfast was hot flat Arab bread and fried eggs, eaten with the fingers. As we ate, Chris explained how the hospital and clinic worked and that I would be here for a week. He was in charge of the hospital and was consulted by GPs working in the out-patient clinic and emergency room, but he spent most of his time organising the ongoing building and conversion.

Chris was so busy that I was left to fit in where I could. I decided to get stuck in straight away. I went first to the emergency room, a small room containing two couches, a cupboard with a broken glass front, and some shelves bearing bandages, drip fluids, splints and antiseptics. The floor was muddy from people's boots. I stitched up a few wounds caused by broken glass and then attached myself to Dr Maher, one of the Palestinian GPs in the out-patient clinic. Rather overweight, unshaven and dressed in a heavy blue overcoat against the cold, he did not conform to the Western idea of a doctor, but he was very friendly, smiling all the time with his nicotine-stained teeth. He had worked with many foreign volunteers and understood their problems. He was thus the ideal person to work with during this first week. He also spoke good English.

Despite being cold, dirty and cramped, the out-patient clinic was seeing 150 patients per day. Some of them – Lebanese women and children, a few Turks – came into the camp from outside. I was surprised that such an unsophisticated clinic would take in patients from outside the camp, but Dr Maher explained that the Palestine Red Crescent Society runs the Palestinian health services as a national health service. Patients are not charged and no one is turned away, regardless of nationality or religion. Almost all of the other health services in Lebanon and Beirut are privately run, so the poor people living around the camps come in to the clinic. There they know they will not be turned away but will get a proper medical examination for no charge. Medicines are also free.

The clinic ran from 8 a.m. to 2 p.m., and after a morning treating people with rheumatic and abdominal pains, colds and bronchitis – their relatives or Dr Maher translating for me – I sat down with Dr Maher in the kitchen upstairs. He told me about his experiences as the doctor in Chatila during the first Camp War (usually referred to as the Ramadan War, because it was fought in the month of Ramadan in May/June 1985). In those days, there were no medical facilities at all in Chatila. The camp was surrounded by the Amal militia and, after the first few days, it was not permitted to transfer the wounded to hospital. The camp residents gathered what few medical supplies they had at home and brought them to Dr Maher, but it amounted to only a little gauze, a few bottles of aspirin and two bottles of Dettol. 'I cleaned and dressed the wounds as best I could,' he said, 'but told the wounded: "When your wound has stopped bleeding please give me back the dressing because I have to use it again."'

He had known he could do very little in the way of physical treatment and many of his patients had died, but he had provided pyschological support by staying with the dying and injured, talking to them to distract them when their pain became too bad and moving them when the fighting made it necessary. At first he had looked after the wounded in the mosque but, when it too came under fire, he moved them to a safer place. On two occasions the Amal militia penetrated the camp and came close to where they were sheltering. Once he heard them in the next-door house and had to do a swift evacuation.

The Palestine Red Crescent Society had been running a big hospital, Gaza Hospital, just outside Chatila in Sabra, but it was looted and burned during that first month's war. Some of the staff and patients had been killed, others had fled, and now it was completely empty.

I had known some of this recent history before I arrived but now I was hearing for myself the terrible reality of what had happened. These days Dr Maher rarely left the camp, preferring to stay and live in the staff residence, rather than go home to his wife and young children who lived outside the camp. 'If something like that happens again,' he said, 'I want to be with my people, not stranded outside.'

After the destruction of Gaza Hospital, the PRCS realised that in order to provide medical care for their people in the camps they would have to establish at least basic emergency hospital facilities inside their boundaries. Having lost all the equipment from Gaza Hospital, with their own doctors and nurses scattered or killed, and the Lebanese staff unable or reluctant to transfer to the camps, they made an appeal for outside help. The appeal reached Europe and MAP sent its first team of six health workers, led by Dr Swee Chai Ang.

'We felt so vulnerable in Chatila during that first attack,' Dr Maher told me. 'We weren't expecting it and were taken by surprise. During the first few days, scores of people were killed until we managed to smuggle arms into the camp and organise a defence.

'Most of the fighting was done by schoolboys. And even some of the women. One day a young man came to me and asked, "Please Dr Maher, I need a bomb. Do you have one?" "I am a doctor," I told him, "I do not have bombs. Why do you need it?" The man explained that he had seen a group of Amal militiamen in a house in the camp. He went off but came back after 20 minutes, laughing. He had not found a bomb, but had picked up a round stone and thrown it into the room. The militiamen had thought it was a hand-grenade and had scattered.'

Strolling around the camp with Dr Maher in the early evening, I was introduced to a tall, thin youth of perhaps 17, with light-brown curly hair. He blushed and smiled shyly as he shook my hand. 'This is the boy who threw the stone,' Dr Maher told me proudly.

The next day I got the first real case of my own. Going round the ward with Chris Giannou I met three-year-old Omar, who had fallen and broken his thigh two days previously. His family did not live in the camp, but had brought him to the hospital because they had heard of Dr Giannou's skill and were too poor to pay for private treatment. Chris had hung him up in 'gallows traction', a technique whereby elastoplast bandages with strings attached are stuck to the skin of the legs to suspend the patient with his bottom just off the bed. The boy would have to stay like this for four weeks until the fracture had mended, but because it was not always easy for them to get through the military checkpoints into the camp, the boy's family had expressed the wish to take him home and look after him there.

Chris turned to me and said, 'Pauline, could you go with them and find something to tie him up to at home?'

'OK,' I said nervously. I was worried, not only because I had never done anything like this before, but also because, frankly, I found the prospect of going alone into the centre of Beirut rather alarming. But Chris seemed confident I would manage and I knew I had to.

We would have to maintain the traction on a splint for the five-kilometre journey, and as we didn't have a conventional splint, I made one with a heavily padded slab of plaster of Paris that had previously been used on someone else. I carried the boy the 75 metres to the edge of the camp where his parents were waiting with an old Mercedes taxi. It had not been easy, stumbling through the crowded alleyways, and the little boy had suffered some pain, but once we set off on the journey in the car towards the city his tears stopped and he quietened down.

We were waved through three or four militia checkpoints during the five-kilometre journey into the city. At each, there was a small group of men filtering the cars into single file by means of old tyres laid in the road. The men were all dressed in military fatigues and heavily armed. At some checkpoints there were tanks or artillery.

Chatila remained under semi-siege, with Amal check-points all around, and it was difficult for the Palestinians, especially the young men, to move in and out. Some of those known to have fought in the first Camp War six months before still never ventured to the perimeter of the camp.

Then we came to an area four or five blocks from the seafront where there were several large hotels, including the tall white Holiday Inn, all of them deserted, their windows smashed and their walls bearing the scars of battle. As we turned away from the sea and up a hill, I saw on the summit a tall, bare brick building, with most of its windows bricked up or sandbagged. It looked strangely sinister. When I got back to the camp I asked about it and was told it was the infamous Murr Tower, planned as a block of flats but never finished. The building overlooked a wide area, and had been used since 1975 as a sniper position and prison. It had changed hands several times but was now under the control of Amal and was commonly thought to contain several hundred prisoners, many of them Palestinians taken during the first Camp War. From then on I always felt un-comfortable passing the Murr Tower, as if I was in some-body's gunsights.

Down the other side of the hill, the car weaved between six-metre-high piles of sand and a lorry container lying on its side and we entered a street called Riad Solh. After 50 metres we turned into a side alley, through a car-park and into a small courtyard. Omar's father said something and his brother, the boy's uncle, translated for me. 'He said that a man was found dead in the car-park this morning.'

Around the courtyard were elegant old colonial-style buildings of yellow sandstone with red-tiled roofs and wooden-shuttered windows, but they were very dilapidated and the courtyard was littered with rubbish and ankle-deep

16

in mud. We picked our way around the edge of the mud, stepped over a low stone wall, climbed up a makeshift wooden stairway, crossed over an alley on a shaky wire-mesh bridge, climbed up some more broken wooden stairs and entered a building. It was no wonder the boy had fallen and broken his leg. The interior was a surprise: there were marble stairs and beautifully patterned tiled floors. The house had been a hotel, but had been deserted by its owners. It was now squatted by poor families.

In one of the rooms occupied by the boy's family I found some coat hooks on the wall. We put a bed underneath and with an extra length of string I fixed up his traction. I showed the parents how to check his buttocks were just off the bed by putting a hand underneath his bottom, and told them that if there were any problems they were to contact us in Chatila.

When I got back to the camp I told Dr Maher where I'd been. He seemed rather surprised and uneasy about me going so close to the Green Line. 'In future,' he said, 'be very careful and go only in the mornings.' There was a sort of unofficial curfew in most of the city and in some areas people could go about their daily business in the morning, but by early evening only the militias were on the streets, when there tended to be more fighting and unrest. Anyone moving about after dark aroused suspicion.

That evening Lieve and the two Palestinian nurses I had met before came up and we had supper of hummus, olives, fried eggs, potatoes and flat Arab bread. The bread is like a pancake and you use it to pick up the food, knives and forks being regarded as unnecessary for most dishes. They showed me how to tear the bread into pieces and use it to pick up mouthfuls of food. Despite many mishaps at first, especially if oil or sauce were served, when I inevitably dripped it on to my clothes, I came to enjoy eating in this way and eventually thought myself quite expert at making the little envelopes of bread which prevented the juices dribbling out all over me. After the meal, Arab tea was brought to us by Rabiha, one of the staff in the hospital kitchen. A quiet, affectionate woman in her early forties, she wore a headscarf like most of the women. Rabiha sat down with us and, although she said little and rarely laughed, she seemed friendly. I discovered that she lived in the staff residence, sleeping where she could find a bed, because her house had been destroyed in the fighting.

The two young Palestinian nurses were, by contrast, vivacious and inquisitive. They were delighted to find someone with whom they could practise their English and, having established already that I was not married, wanted to know why not, whether my brother and sister were married, whether I wanted to get married and have children and, if so, how many. I think they felt rather sorry for my being on the shelf and they promised to find me a Palestinian husband.

In turn, I wanted to learn Arabic and Dr Maher offered to give me lessons. We began there and then and I wrote down phonetically the Arabic words in my notebook. The lessons with Dr Maher were unstructured and informal and in his enthusiasm he always told me more words than I could possibly remember at one sitting; but they were extremely useful because he taught me not only common, basic conversational Arabic, but the vocabulary necessary for dealing with patients. This I could never have learned from books because, throughout the Arab world, there are many different dialects, each group with its own street language which is different from the standard written Arabic. During that first lesson, the evening exchanges of gunfire and shells across the Green Line, about two kilometres east of Chatila, rattled and rumbled in the background.

The next day, in view of my experience of plastic surgery, Chris Giannou asked me to see a patient. He was a young man who had been tortured by the Christian Phalangist militia four years before. The torture had scarred the palmar surface of his right index finger and he could no longer straighten it. Luckily, the scarring was only on the surface and the tendons were not affected, so it was easily correctable by a simple technique called z-plasties.

I performed the operation in the emergency room, using a local anaesthetic, and splinted the finger straight. I told him he was to keep the splint on until the finger was well healed and even then to wear it at night for at least six weeks. He promised to comply and I was sure he would because I had guessed that the inability to straighten his right index finger had not only inconvenienced him in everyday activities, but it was his trigger finger and he could not shoot. I decided it was not my business to judge the reasons he wanted the correction; my job was to treat him in the best way I could.

The next morning Sol-Britt drove me in the NORWAC ambulance down towards Riad Solh to visit Omar. We missed the car-park entrance and took the next turning 30 metres further on, hoping to come round to the other side of the hotel. But instead we entered a maze of dark, dirty, narrow streets. Some of the old buildings were derelict. Some were still occupied and trade was still evident amongst the decay: cars being fixed, small, seedy cafés, half-boarded-up corner shops. The people looked out at us from their doorways with suspicion and a touch of menace. This was the area of the old commercial centre, the souks and markets, now on the edge of the Green Line and a no-go area, devoid of any law or control. Few people came here unless they had some shady business.

We seemed to be going deeper into the labyrinth, so we stopped and timidly asked the way from a man standing in the doorway of a café. I showed the man the address on a card from the old hotel that Omar's uncle had given me. We explained that we were health workers going to visit a sick child. He looked us over suspiciously and I was glad I had kept on my doctor's white coat. Sol-Britt and I kept smiling sweetly and after what seemed like an age he smiled back and offered to show us the way. He climbed into the back of the ambulance and directed us through a couple of alleys and into the familiar car-park from the other side, then he got out and disappeared with a wave.

Omar seemed to be content and was obviously being well cared for. His parents were keeping him clean, warm and happy. I gave Omar an apple I had brought so he would not only associate me with interference and pain, and adjusted his traction slightly. We drank the customary cup of thick sweet coffee and then left. It was a relief to get back inside the camp; the people were friendly there and I felt safe and secure.

That evening, while I ate with Chris Giannou in his room, I plied him with questions about war surgery. He not only told me a wealth of technical details to do with operations, which complemented the knowledge I had picked up from books before I arrived, but, more importantly, how to make the most of what we had available. He explained how to give an autotransfusion (giving the patient back his own lost blood); how to operate without conventional anaesthetics; how to best clean instruments without a steriliser. Above all, he stressed that I should never throw away anything which in England would be classed as disposable but which it might be possible to use again.

A friend of Chris's whom I met in Cyprus on the way to Beirut, and who had once shared a room with him at university, had warned me that if I ever asked Chris a question, I had better have sandwiches with me because his answers were renowned for their detail. I remained spellbound until late into the night as he told me his experiences during the seven or eight years he had worked in the Lebanon. During the 1982 Israeli invasion he had been working in a hospital in Saida, south of Beirut. The Israeli troops arrived in the middle of an operation and ordered him to down tools. They arrested him along with the other Palestinian hospital staff and kept him in prison in Israel for three weeks before releasing him at the request of the Canadian authorities.

During our conversation Chris smoked Gitanes one after another. He kept offering them to me and eventually I accepted one. It was my first cigarette for four years, and it was a mistake.

I was having an Arabic lesson with Dr Maher the following evening when the gunfire and shelling suddenly became much louder. Whenever I heard gunfire I would ask where it came from, so that I could learn to judge the distances. The answer was always: 'A long way away' or 'Green Line'. Even when I could tell that the shooting was closer I was always told it was far away. In the end I asked why they were not telling me the truth. A young man answered that if I were told it was closer I might be frightened and they did not want me to worry. But tonight Dr Maher was very tense, playing with his prayer-beads and stopping to listen to each explosion and crack of sniper fire. The fighting was happening around the perimeter of the camp some 75 metres away from us. He told me not to go on the roof and that if it came any closer we were to go downstairs. After half an hour, however, it died away and Dr Maher relaxed.

The lesson ended and I went to my room. On the way, I looked into the kitchen and found Rabiha, the kindly hospital cook. She was slumped on a chair, weeping. I sat down beside her. 'What's the matter?' I asked. She explained in broken English that she was crying for her son. 'My son is gone. He is 17 years old. He was in the Ramadan War. He is my only son. I hear nothing. But he is in Syria.' Later, Lieve told me that this was wishful thinking. Rabiha's son was almost certainly dead. Some boys claimed to have seen his body, but Rabiha could not accept it and often wept for him. Divorced, her home destroyed, living under threat in Chatila and mourning the loss of her only child, she was desperately alone.

There was gunfire and shelling again the following day, audible intermittently throughout the day, well outside the camp. Two days before, a peace plan had been instituted in West Beirut to try to prevent a repetition of the Flag War. It was decided to put representatives of the PSP, Amal militia and the official Lebanese Army together at each checkpoint, but squabbling began again after 48 hours.

The next day was Saturday and Dirk, Lieve and I set off with Barbara to Sour in South Lebanon for a meeting with the other NORWAC staff working there. We hailed a 'service' taxi in the street outside Chatila to take us to Cola, the gathering place for people travelling to the south. Service taxis were communal, picking up people and dropping them off on the way between certain fixed points in the city. They were not marked as taxis but were easily recognised as the most dilapidated Mercedes drifting along in the nearside lanes hooting for custom. Dirt cheap, charging a standard fare of about 10p, and extremely numerous, they were very efficient. I never had to wait for one longer than a minute.

Cola roundabout, under the feet of a flyover no longer used because its other end was deep in the city's Green Line danger zone, was a wonderful scene of noisy, bustling chaos. A completely anarchic version of Hyde Park Corner, the traffic went round it in both directions at once. Service taxis hooted, dropping off and picking up passengers. The dozens of taxis going south parked haphazardly around the south-facing slip road, narrowing the roadway. Beside them stood their drivers shouting the names of their destinations: 'Saida, Saida, Saida,' 'Sour, Sour, Sour,' each car moving off as it filled up. Some of the buildings near the roundabout were half collapsed, relics of the 1982 Israeli invasion; on the pavement were handcarts selling sandwiches, tinned fizzy drinks, cigarettes, fruit and cheap household items.

The others laughed when, with a typically British belief in the virtue of queueing, I suggested the taxi men might do better with some signs and tickets issued on a first come, first served basis. Anyway, I was wrong of course, for the system worked very well and within five minutes we were on our way to Sour. The fare for the 60-kilometre journey was also cheap at about £1 each. The sun was shining brightly, bringing the temperature up to 60°F, and as we sped down the coast road I had time to relax and think over my first week in the Lebanon.

The tension on the streets of West Beirut, where the authority of the state was virtually nil and the power was in the hands of the paramilitary militias, contrasted with the sense of personal safety inside the Palestinian refugee camps. Right from the very start I felt I could breathe freely and relax every time I entered the narrow paths within the confines of the camps. I was appalled at the material poverty, overcrowding and physical hardships of life in the refugee camps and in the poorer areas of the city, but comforted by the extraordinary hospitality of the people, their curiosity about and friendliness to strangers.

When we arrived in Sour, a large town on the coast, we went straight to the flat rented by NORWAC in the Palestinian camp of Bourj al Chemali. This camp housed around 10,000 people a kilometre south-east of Sour itself. The two-bedroomed NORWAC flat, on the first floor of a two-storey house, was light and airy, and from the flat roof above one could look out over the fields of olive trees, banana plantations and orange groves to the sea, or down into the camp at children teasing a goat or playing happily with kittens in the small gardens. Relationships between the Palestinians and the Shiite population were good, the confrontation around the Beirut camps had not extended to here and the atmosphere was very peaceful compared to the simmering menace of Beirut.

After an evening meal of spaghetti and salad in the flat,

the seven of us – ourselves, Sol-Britt, and NORWAC workers Gunnar and Anne – sat down on the mattresses on the floor, Arab style, and discussed how we would divide up our work. It was decided that Dirk and I would join Barbara at Bourj al Barajneh. Dirk would begin working in the clinic, and I was to start in surgery at Haifa Hospital. Lieve would carry on in the primary health centre in Chatila. Anne, a British midwife who had arrived in the Lebanon with me, would stay in Sour, working three days a week with Gunnar in a local Lebanese village called Chaabiye and three days a week in another village, Quasmiye, until a new team arrived from Sweden the following week to work in the local villages.

Chapter 2

On Monday morning I started work in Haifa Hospital in Bourj al Barajneh camp. I was given my own room with its own toilet and shower and luxurious hot water. The room contained a bed, a table and sofa and a rickety cupboard. I dumped my bags on the bed and went on a tour of the hospital with Dr Mounir, one of the Palestinian junior surgeons working there. Six months before the first Camp War, Haifa Hospital, an L-shaped building of five storeys including the basement, had been a rehabilitation centre for the handicapped. Now it was undergoing conversion into a general and emergency surgical hospital. The top two floors had been damaged by the fighting and were not in use yet, but in the basement a complex of emergency room, X-ray room, laboratory and operating-theatre was functioning and had worked reasonably well during a 10-day clash in September. On the ground floor, the four wards each containing three beds were occasionally admitting patients – today there were four in-patients – but the conversion work on the first floor was not completed.

Equipment in the hospital was sparse, old and primitive and there was an air of despondent inertia amongst the staff. Most had worked in the modern Gaza Hospital and their morale had been shattered by its destruction. Dr Mounir himself had been in surgical training with several other junior surgeons under the supervision of two Lebanese professors of surgery. All that was now lost. He was depressed in Haifa and blamed the bosses of the Palestine Red Crescent Society for not upgrading the hospital faster and for treating the Palestinian doctors in a dictatorial fashion. There were six Palestinian doctors working in Haifa at that time, three in surgery, one in orthopaedics and two GPs, working in morning clinics and with an on-call system. 'How often are out-patient clinics held?' I asked him. 'Oh, every day,' he replied. 'So when are the operating lists?' I asked. 'Whenever there is an operation.' It sounded hopelessly inefficient. Ward rounds were sporadic, patients' admission notes were not kept. I made a number of suggestions as to how the organisation of the hospital might be improved. Each one drew the same response: 'Yes, we used to do that in Gaza.'

I went to bed that night feeling slightly depressed, only to be woken at 3 a.m. by the noise of gunfire, followed by the sound of running feet. I rushed downstairs. A young man had been shot at the edge of the camp. One bullet had grazed his skull just above his ear and another had ricocheted off the ground as he ran, passing through the sole of his foot and shattering the bones. Dr Mounir, the duty doctor, called for the anaesthetic technician living in the camp. Then he and I took the wounded man to the operating-theatre. The scalp wound was minor but we took a long time picking out the bone splinters and fragments of bullet from his foot.

I fell back into bed at 5 a.m., but my room was between two wards and there was so much noisy to-ing and fro-ing all night long that I slept only briefly. In the morning I had an upset stomach, was unable to eat breakfast and felt sick and faint whilst performing an appendicectomy. I limped down to the NORWAC clinic, where Barbara worked, and slept well that night. But the upset stomach continued and after yet another sleepless night in the noisy hospital I was almost in a state of collapse. During an operation on Thursday morning I felt so weak that I had to sit down.

That evening I sat silently with Barbara in the NORWAC clinic. One of her closest friends in the camp was about to leave for a job in the Gulf, and she was gloomy. The rain and cold weather were back again with a vengeance. The electricity had gone off. I was desperately tired and still feeling sick. As I huddled under a couple of damp blankets I felt miserable and pathetic. If I couldn't cope with this, I thought, what would I be like when fighting broke out. Maybe I should pack up now and go home to the comforts of England. But then I reminded myself that I had not come to Lebanon expecting it to be all jolly fun. Things would get better. I just had to stick it out. And if morale and organisation were bad, I must try to improve them.

As the only qualified surgeon in Haifa, I was put in charge of the surgery department. I made a number of suggestions for improvements: daily ward rounds, better clinical notes, formal times for out-patient clinics and operating lists, requests for new equipment, weekly lectures by myself and others. But although the other doctors politely agreed with my ideas, few were put into operation. Still, I managed to do some work. I had brought with me a skin-graft knife. The hospital did not have one, so I was able to put skin-grafts on patients waiting for them. The first to come in was a thirteen-year-old girl called Suzanne who needed a re-vision of a scar on her foot which prevented her from wear-ing shoes. It worked well, and when it healed she came in again, delighted, and showed me her new shoes.

The hospital was staffed by 30 nurses, both male and female, working in shifts of 10. Not all of them were fully trained. There were also 10 administrative staff, led by a woman called Nidal, and 10 domestic workers, most of them women. In addition, there were a few porters.

All the staff were welcoming and friendly and it was from them that I got my first lessons in Palestinian customs and hospitality. Almost every day, at the end of a morning's work, Hassan, one of the operating-theatre nurses, would say to me, 'Do you have anything more to do now?' If I answered, 'No,' he would say, 'Good, then you can visit my family with me.'

Traditionally, you honour a family by visiting them. Strangers are especially welcome and offered the best hospitality the family can afford. The longer you stay and the more you eat and drink, the greater the honour to the family, so we were often feasted until we protested that it was impossible to squeeze in another slice of the apples or oranges which were peeled for us in abundance at the end of a meal. It was rather humbling to be treated so well. We in Britain, I reflected, are not always so courteous to foreigners, sometimes quite the reverse. Even to make a home visit to a patient could be time-consuming because it was rude not to accept tea or coffee, and it had to be a matter of life or death to leave without drinking something, even in the poorest houses.

Once I made a visit in late evening to a young man with bronchitis, who was lying in bed in a four-metre-square room in which 13 other people were also sleeping on mattresses on a bare earth floor. The whole family lived in that little room, from the grandmother in her eighties to the youngest grandchild of 18 months. During the day, the mattresses were piled up in one corner so that the room could be used. But even here I was coerced into drinking coffee. Such abject poverty and overcrowding was not uncommon in the camp and the diseases associated with it were also in evidence – TB, scabies, lice and, especially amongst the children, diarrhoea. The United Nations Relief and Works Agency had been set up in 1949 as a temporary body to meet the needs of the Palestinian refugees, but with dwindling funds UNRWA was unable to cope with their present needs and the Palestinians had instituted a social welfare system of their own. Pensions for widows and the disabled, and orphanages called Beit Atfal Samoud ('Home for the Children of the Steadfast') were funded largely by contributions from Palestinians making money in the Gulf or elsewhere.

The material poverty also belied the educational and

professional achievements of the inhabitants. Dentists, engineers, teachers, doctors, craftsmen and tradesmen were living in the lowliest of homes and in drastically impoverished surroundings. Many were unemployed. Hassan explained that those few who had managed to obtain a Lebanese work permit to work outside the camp since the first Camp War had lost their jobs because they were unable to move out of the camps, either afraid of, or in danger from, fighting in the streets. Work inside the camps was scarce. Some of the men were paid a small wage as reserve fighters, but most of the families depended on money sent by relatives working in the Gulf, Europe or America.

In the first few days at Bourj al Barajneh I began to get a sense of the geography and culture of the camp. Bourj al Barajneh refugee camp is a sort of shanty town of about 500 by 400 metres. On one side, the east side, the camp buildings face the apartment buildings of the mainly Shiite southern suburbs across a street. To the west runs the airport road, parallel to the edge of the camp and separated from it by 50 metres of waste ground with only a few scattered houses, now mainly deserted, and the low-walled camp cemetery which juts out 40 metres from the camp, almost reaching the airport road. The other two sides, north and south, are separated from the surrounding buildings by between 30 and 50 metres of open waste ground, most of which had been produced during the first rounds of the Camp War in 1985 when the Amal militia dynamited the houses at the edge of the camp. Apart from the dirt road leading to the hospital from the airport road entrance and another dirt road from the south 50 metres into the camp, there were no roads wide enough for cars. The only way through the camp was on foot through the labyrinth of narrow alleys one to two metres wide, mostly paved unevenly with concrete, with open drainage channels running along and across them and waterpipes crossing at ankle height and, in places, shell craters up to a metre across and 30 centimetres deep. I always wondered why more people did not fall and twist their ankles but I suppose that most, like me, were aware that one had to look down all the time until one knew the ways by heart. In many of the alleys were small one-room shops and stalls selling most household items, general stores, greengrocers', butchers' and a few pastry stalls. Ten metres from the door of the clinic was Abu Khalil's juice stall where he made and sold fresh banana milk, carrot juice, orange juice and strawberry juice.

The houses – of one, two or three storeys, gradually replacing the tents in the 1950s and 1960s, were built of breeze-block and plaster, mostly painted white and all pock-marked with bullet and shrapnel holes. Some of the poorer houses still had corrugated iron roofs. Many of the front doors were open during the day for the children to run in and out, and to welcome visitors or passers-by. Many women made their own bread and the delicious smell drifted out into the alleyways.

I decided to pay another visit to Omar, the boy with the broken thigh. Lieve said she would come with me in the ambulance but when we reached the street before Riad Solh we heard gunfire. We stopped and a man told us that the shooting was in Riad Solh Square, just 100 metres from where we were going. He offered to take us: 'I will drive the ambulance, and we will go very fast and everything will be all right.' Lieve and I looked at each other and said, 'No, thank you.' We listened for a couple of minutes but the shooting seemed to be getting closer, so we turned round and came home.

A few weeks before Christmas a new face appeared in Bourj al Barajneh. Ben Alofs, a Dutch nurse, returned from a month in Holland. He worked with Barbara in the clinic and she seemed very relieved at his return. A tall man in his early thirties, with a broad smile, he spoke passable Arabic, having worked in the Lebanon on and off during the four years since the Israeli invasion of 1982. Ben was very popular in the camp, especially with the children, who would call to him all the time, 'Ben! Ben! Ben!' Sometimes it sounded like an emergency, but when he turned to them they would just wave and call merrily, 'Hello!' Heralded by the shouting of the children, we often knew he was arriving at the clinic before we saw him.

Ben was very knowledgeable about the conflict in the Lebanon and in the weeks that followed he tried to explain the complex history of the 10-year-old Lebanese civil war.

The conflict was both political and religious, essentially Lebanese but with the influence of foreign powers. Apart from the occasional influx of refugees – Armenians, Kurds and more recently Palestinians – the same five Lebanese communities have co-existed in the region for hundreds of years. Two of them are Christian, the Maronites and the Greeks (Orthodox and Catholic); the other three are Muslim – the Shiites, the Sunnis and the Druze. These communities are separated by culture, religion and sectarian loyalty. The unbreakable link between politics and religion was reinforced by the French. Under their mandate from 1920 to 1943, the new state of Greater Lebanon was created from part of the old Ottoman province of Syria and incorporated Mount Lebanon, which brought the five communities together. The President would always be a Maronite Christian, the Prime Minister always a Sunni Muslim, the Speaker of the House a Shiite Muslim, and the parliamentary seats divided between Christians and Muslims in a 6:5 ratio. These posts were allocated according to the size of each community in the total population. Thus the Maronite Christians, being the single largest community, were given the most powerful positions. The whole structure, supposed to ensure representation of all groups, in fact preserved the supremacy of the Christians even when the Muslims with their larger families became the majority. Discontented Muslims, mainly Shiite, migrated from the poor rural regions of Lebanon and settled in the sprawling suburbs of Beirut, hoping to find work. Also in this belt of shanty towns were the Palestinians – mostly Sunni Muslims – in their refugee camps. They sympathised with the demands of the poor for political reform and in turn were supported in their demands to return to their homeland.

Tensions grew. In February 1975 a Nasserite leader was assassinated and in April a busload of 27 Palestinians were killed in Ain el Rumanieh, a suburb of East Beirut, by the extreme right-wing Christian Phalangist militia. These killings sparked a series of armed confrontations which rapidly escalated into large-scale battles between the right-wing Christians and the broad-left non-sectarian Lebanese National Movement. Syria was drawn in on the side of the Christians. A year later, an estimated 50,000 were dead as a result of the fighting and a kilometre-wide strip of destruction through the centre of the city, the 'Green Line', divided the mainly Christian East, from the mainly Muslim West, Beirut. When I arrived in 1985, divisions had deepened after 10 years of strife, and the new generation of adults had grown up in an atmosphere of bloody vengeance and bitterness.

The old feudal lords had always been protected by their own small private armies. Some of these developed into paramilitary armies or 'militias' and, as tensions grew and clashes spread, new militias appeared. The Christian Phalange militia was modelled on Europe's fascists. Pierre Gemayel, father of the present-day President, went to the Olympic Games in Berlin in 1936. He was so impressed by Hitler and his Nazis that on his return to the Lebanon he set up the Phalangist militia. Their stronghold is in East Beirut. I was bewildered at first because the Phalangists are also known as 'Lebanese Forces'. They are not to be confused with the official Lebanese Army, which has brigades drawn from all the different sects. The militias are entirely separate from the official army.

Kamal Jumblatt, leader of the Druze before his son Walid

Jumblatt, tried to create a non-sectarian broad-based socialist group (and partly succeeded) in the Progressive Socialist Party (PSP), to which most of the Druze belong. Its heartland is the Chouf Mountains, but it also controls part of West Beirut.

Amal was set up in 1974 by Imam Musa Sadr, a Muslim Shiite religious man who later disappeared in Libya in 1978. A movement of the dispossessed Shiites, it was called Amal ('Hope') in 1976. In 1980 the leadership was taken over by Nabih Berri. Amal is now Syria's closest ally in Lebanon.

Hezbollah, or Party of God, is a Shiite fundamentalist Muslim militia, and aligns itself more closely with Iran. It emerged in the early 1980s and is now gaining some ground as Shiites, disaffected with Amal, leave to join Hezbollah.

The strength of Hezbollah and Amal lies in the southern suburbs of West Beirut, the south of Lebanon and parts of the Bekaa valley.

There are other militias belonging to the Sunni Muslim groups: the Murabitoun in West Beirut, the Tawheed in Tripoli in the north of Lebanon, and the Nasserists in Saida. Also there is the non-sectarian Lebanese Communist Party whose leader is George Hawi.

The reasons for the Camp War were not clear to me, and everybody had their own explanation, but in conversations two definite and interlinked reasons emerged. The key was Syria. The Lebanon had gradually broken up into armed 'cantons' (states within a state), controlled by the various militias. Those Palestinian camps involved in the Camp War were in the area controlled by the Amal. Syria, wanting allies in Lebanon to extend its own influence, had supported the rise to power of the Amal militia since its inception in 1974. Furthermore, Syria wanted to eliminate the political power base in the camps of the PLO leader Yasser Arafat, who urged a negotiated solution for the Palestinians, and to replace it with support for the more intransigent pro-Syrian factions in the camps.

In 1983, Syria managed to enlist the support of the pro-Syrian anti-Arafat Palestinians in Tripoli in the north of Lebanon and, after a bloody battle in the camps and the city, had forced Arafat to leave. The memory of Palestinian fighting Palestinian was still an open wound in the minds of many and they swore never to repeat such a catastrophe.

Early in 1985, the Amal militia – with the approval of the Syrians – attacked the camps of Sabra and Chatila and Bourj al Barajneh in southern Beirut. As Amal knew, the camps were unprepared for an attack; they thought they would take them over in a matter of days. But the Palestinians consolidated their defences and despite heavy losses were not defeated. After a month the Amal militia were forced to give up.

Most of the adult men in the camps had been evacuated as PLO fighters in 1982. With the fighting men gone and despite an international guarantee of safety for civilians, somewhere between 1,000 and 3,000 Palestinians, mostly women, children and old men, had been slaughtered in the camps of Sabra and Chatila by the Christian Phalangist militia, while the Israeli Army lit up the camps with flares and looked on.

After the recent sudden attack by the Amal militia, the Palestinian men had visions of another such slaughter. The pain and guilt of the 1982 massacre had not gone from their minds and, determined not to leave their families un-protected, many of the men drifted back from abroad into the camps and more arms were smuggled in. The influx increased when, in the summer of 1985, Amal procured from Syria artillery, mortars and tanks.

Some Palestinians left the Beirut camps after that and some still wanted to go. 'But where *can* I go?' I heard more than once. Some went to families in other camps and a few to families living outside the camps, but that was also dangerous. Amal had entered the homes of Palestinians living outside the camps in the first war and many were evicted or killed. This had, in fact, strengthened many Palestinians' resolve to stay in the camps. 'I will stay here and die defending my family,' one young man told me, 'rather than be cut down like a dog in the street.'

One afternoon in late December, a fifteen-year-old boy was rushed into the emergency room in Haifa Hospital by frantic stretcher-bearers. He had been shot in the head by a handgun. There was a large open wound on the left side of his head, exposing the brain, and he was paralysed down the right side. He was still semi-conscious and after re-suscitating him with a drip and drugs we decided to transfer him to the American University Hospital in the city where I knew they had a modern neurosurgery department.

The Lebanese Red Cross came with an ambulance and I went with him to the hospital. The twenty-minute journey was a nightmare. Driving at high speed through the traffic with sirens blaring, once smashing into a traffic bollard, we were thrown around in the back of the ambulance. I took the skin off my knees skidding across the floor. Then the injured boy, Jihad, was sick and I had to clean out his mouth with my hand. The American University Hospital was like a big European hospital and the boy was taken quickly through the emergency department to X-ray and then to a computerised brain scanner. This was much more like the hospitals I was used to and for a moment I wished I could have been working in a place like this – but I also felt resentful that the Palestinians did not have such facilities.

I persuaded the neurosurgical registrar to let me in to see the operation and so I was able to watch the cleaning of the brain and closure of the wound by the most experienced experts in the world in this type of injury. The registrar, Dr Jamal Taha, a Lebanese, was polite and chatty and showed me round the complex of 10 operating-theatres, many of them equipped with specialised instruments for eye surgery, cardiac surgery, neurosurgery and orthopaedics. In another theatre an operation was in progress on a bomb-blast victim. Two teams were working together, one on the abdomen and one on the eyes. This was the daily work of these doctors.

As we walked round the hospital, Dr Taha talked sadly about the generation of Lebanese teenagers who had grown up with violence. They had, he said, become indifferent to death. 'They even play Russian roulette.'

'What do you mean?' I asked.

'You know, like in Vietnam. In the last six months I have seen six teenagers admitted to this hospital with gunshot wounds to the head caused by games of Russian roulette. They all died. One day a boy came in and died and the following day his best friend died the same way. Apparently, the fiancée of the first one had asked his friend, "How did he die?" The friend picked up a gun and told her, "Like this", and shot himself in the head.'

I was astonished. 'It's true,' said Dr Taha. 'That is what Beirut is like now. Some games are played for money, some merely for the thrill. We have our own game now, "Lebanese routlette". Boys run across streets known to be exposed to sniper fire. In some places they put mattresses behind sandbanks so that they can dive over to a soft landing.'

Christmas Day is not a Muslim holiday, so I worked in Haifa in the morning. Most people knew it was our major feast day and wished us Merry Christmas. In the afternoon I went down to the clinic where Ben, Barbara, Lieve and Dirk were preparing for Christmas dinner. Ben and Barbara had bought a Christmas tree and decorations in Hamra, the main shopping area of West Beirut, and had even seen Father Christmas there. Santa had been forced to take cover when someone got overexcited.

We decorated the tree and the clinic and sat down on the floor with some young Palestinian friends of Ben and Barbara, to eat our Christmas dinner of chicken and garlic, potatoes and salad and afterwards, oranges, mandarins and bananas. These fruits grew in the winter and were deliciously cheap and fresh.

One of the young men, Thair, often visited the clinic. He spoke excellent English and was a good, enthusiastic storyteller. After our Christmas meal he told us his own story, of how he had travelled to Europe that September hoping to find work and escape the violence in Lebanon.

He went first to West Germany, then with some other Palestinians to Sweden, where, after a week, they were refused permission to stay and sent back to Germany. Naively, he thought this was because he had been in a group. He decided to try again on his own. Because his papers had been marked with a refusal of entry, he was arrested at the airport by a policewoman. 'I could not struggle against a woman,' he explained, 'so I just held out my hands for her to put on the handcuffs. She was very beautiful,' he added as if in explanation.

Thair was taken to prison where he was put in a warm cell with a comfortable bed, a chair and table. He was well fed and even brought an Arabic newspaper. 'Is this prison?' he asked. 'Yes, it is,' said the guard. 'Then, thank you, I will stay here,' said Thair.

When the authorities came to throw him out he refused to leave, but when they returned with three Doberman dogs, he said, 'OK, I will go now.' He went back to West Germany, where he was miserable, unable to get work or a place to stay, discovering that many disillusioned Lebanese and Palestinians were spending the family savings on drink and drugs.

It was when Thair heard news of the 10-day assault on Bourj al Barajneh camp by the Amal militia that he returned to Beirut. He was concerned for his family. But he still had to get into the besieged camp. Outside Beirut airport, putting on a Lebanese accent, he asked a taxi-driver to take him into town, terrified in case they might be stopped at an Amal checkpoint. If the Amal saw his blue

Palestinian identity card, they might kill him. Praying that the taxi-driver was kind, he confessed to being a Palestinian and offered the man all his money, about £20, to take him near to the camp. The driver agreed and dropped him by some deserted buildings. Dodging in and out of empty buildings he finally reached the camp perimeter and dashed across the road to safety.

Thair's story was typical. Many Palestinians in Lebanon dream of finding a new life in the peaceful haven of Europe and think that, if they just arrive there with a willingness to learn and work, everything will be fine. But confronted with a bureaucracy they don't understand, culture shock, racism and a high cost of living, many end up on the streets or crowded into squats and eventually get sent back, their dream shattered and the family savings frittered away.

A few months later, Thair came to work at the clinic. He had no formal duties but he soon made himself indispensable, translating, registering patients and keeping record cards. He was a capable electrician, and even guarded the clinic if we were away on Sundays.

He was scrupulously honest, and a devout Muslim. He was also very interested in us foreigners and our ways. One afternoon he invited us to visit his family – father, mother, brother and sister – for the usual feast. Starters of soup, olives, hummus and other dips, salad and bread. Then rice and chicken, spiced meat, potatoes and tomatoes, all laid out on a large fold-up formica-topped table set up especially for the meal and taking up almost the whole space in the small dining-room. Thair's father was a grey-haired, quiet-spoken teacher, who had learned his fluent English as a child at school in Palestine under British rule. As we ate he described how as a teenager he and his family had been forced to flee from his home village of Tarshiha in northern Palestine in 1948 when the fighting between the Zionists and the Arab armies threatened to engulf them.

The shooting and bombing came closer and closer and,

when news of massacres in Arab villages reached them, they packed a few belongings, locked their front doors and set off on foot. For two days they walked northwards, hiding in ditches from the bombs and the fighting, before crossing the Lebanese border with thousands of other Palestinians who, like them, were convinced that the war would soon be over and they would return to their homes within a few months.

They were never allowed to go home so UNRWA set up refugee camps in Lebanon and the other neighbouring Arab countries to provide temporary shelter for the refugees, and they have lived there ever since, joined by the thousands more who fled in 1967 when Israel took what remained of Palestine, the West Bank and the Gaza Strip.

Thair's father hated Lebanon. 'There is only violence and fear here,' he said. Thirty-nine years later he still kept the front-door key of the family home in Palestine.

'We don't hate the Jews,' he said. 'We lived in peace with the Palestinian Jews before the Zionists came. We hate what the Zionists have done to us.'

Many other families from Tarshiha were living in Bourj al Barajneh – an estimated 40 per cent of the population. They carried on the traditions of village life as best they could, living in extended families, their children marrying the children of respected families from Tarshiha, the parents of the bridegroom providing a home for the young couple, which now usually meant building a new room on the first or second floor of the family home in the cramped and overcrowded camp.

'We felt betrayed by the British,' said Thair's father when he came to the end of his story. 'They handed over their weapons to the Israelis after the partition of Palestine in 1947, then left us at their mercy.'

I knew I had to say something. 'I am sorry that my government has treated you so badly,' I stuttered.

He suddenly realised I was British. 'I'm terribly sorry,' he said. 'I would not have spoken so badly about the British if I'd known. You are our guest. I should not have been so impolite.'

'No, it is we British who owe you an apology,' I said. 'We were responsible for partitioning Palestine to create Israel in 1947. It is the British government that owes the Palestinian people a very great debt, a debt they have not begun to repay.'

But Thair's father was still embarrassed by his imagined *faux pas*. 'Of course, not all British people are responsible for the wrongs done by their government,' he said. 'Even the prophet Mohammed had a wicked uncle.'

Thair's elder brother lived in the USA and the family had not seen him for seven years. 'I can't visit him,' explained the father. 'I have no passport.' Like the two million Palestinians living outside Israel, he had no official nationality – no right to return to his home, no passport and, therefore, no way to escape the poverty of the refugee camp.

I wondered aloud why most of us in Britain knew nothing about these people and the misery of their lives. All we in the West knew about the Palestinians was hijackings, bombings and shootings. Such violent actions harmed these people too, pushing a peaceful solution further from their grasp. Families like Thair's, innocent and forgiving, simply waited, wondering what the hell was going to happen next. They felt they did not belong in Lebanon and their identification of themselves as wholly Palestinian had not altered at all over the years. When we described ourselves as 'foreigners', it often provoked the response, 'We too are foreigners here in Lebanon.' Even the young children born in the camps, if asked where they came from, would answer, 'Tarshiha', 'Kabri', or 'Haifa', the villages and towns from which their families had fled.

After Christmas, Ben came with me to visit Omar. He was well and happy, spinning around actively on his traction. I also visited my other patient, Jihad, in the American University Hospital. He was conscious and out of the intensive-care unit. They had put him in a two-bed ward next to an eighteen-year-old who had been shot in the back and had been in hospital for one and a half years. Jihad could not speak or move his right arm or leg at all, but his mother and family were effusively grateful to me, pressing sweet, nutty pastries, sticky with honey, into my hands and thanking me for saving him. I tried to tell them that I had done very little; indeed, to my mind, the only thing of value I had done was to prevent him from choking on his own vomit on the way to the hospital.

On New Year's Eve, we had a small party in the NORWAC clinic. Thair came with a few friends, Ben cooked some traditional Dutch apple-doughnuts and we danced to Arab and Western music. New Year's Eve is a holiday in Lebanon too, celebrated in typical fashion by loosing off about 10 million bullets into the sky at midnight. Thair and his friends told me that it was wise to stay inside, because the bullets rained down again. Nevertheless, at midnight we all went on to the small balcony upstairs in the clinic and watched thousands of lines of glowing red tracer bullets streaming up into the night sky.

Work in the hospital was improving. Clinics and operating lists were fixed on separate days and weekly lectures organised. There was a new director of the hospital, a Palestinian woman called Dr Iklas. Um Walid, the chief of the PRCS, whom Barbara referred to as 'the Queen', had removed the previous director and appointed a new one. The change-over had been completed within a few days without anyone being consulted. Dr Iklas was a short, dark, chubby woman, honest and well-meaning, but very junior and unambitious. She had only recently qualified in the USSR and had no administrative experience. Um Walid had given her the job because she was not a 'troublemaker'. Although she was provided with an expensive new desk with a smart leather top and writing-pad as befitted her status, she knew that her appointment over the heads of much more senior staff would breed resentment. I occasionally saw her sitting alone in her office, staring across the top of the empty desk. This assignment of status according to the lavishness of someone's office furniture rather than on merit I disliked intensely. You can see the 'big desk syndrome' all over the world and it is thoroughly contemptible. I thought of Chris Giannou living in Chatila between piles of onions and sacks of flour with no desk or office, and providing excellent surgical care in the most adverse, austere conditions.

I felt the vulnerability of Dr Iklas. I too was vulnerable. I was an outsider, holder of the coveted FRCS (Fellowship of the Royal College of Surgeons), which Dr Mounir, the junior surgeon who had first showed me round the hospital, had once tried to obtain but, having run out of money, had had to give up. I was constantly aware of my lack of experience in dealing with bullet and shrapnel wounds and my inability to speak the language. I had an inkling that I too had been 'placed' in Haifa to quell subversion. Although I sympathised with the junior doctors, their opposition to ideas for improvement and the way they constantly tried to undermine Dr Iklas I found destructive and did not like.

Dr Iklas was straightforward and honourable, and whenever she asked for my support I gave it. In turn, she was a great help to me. On the evenings when she was the duty doctor she shared my room, and when she wasn't working we would talk late into the night. She explained why the other doctors were so disillusioned, why they resented her, even why some of them resented me. Through her eyes, I gained a better understanding of the little world in which I worked.

Dr Iklas also had the support of Nidal, the hospital's chief administrator. She was an impressive, rather austere-looking woman in her forties. Extremely efficient and hard-working, Nidal had been a loyal employee of the PRCS for 15 years and we were very lucky to have her at Haifa Hospital.

In the end Dr Iklas asked to be relieved of the responsibility of being director and returned to clinical work.

Chapter 3

January 1986 was very wet and cold in Haifa, but at least I was sleeping much better. I now put cotton wool in my ears every night. I made a final visit to Omar, the little boy with the broken thigh. We did an X-ray in Chatila which showed that the bone was healing well in a perfect position. He was released from traction.

Jihad too was making good progress. His head wound had healed, he was smiling and he was able to utter a few slurred words; he had even recovered a little movement in his right leg. The American University Hospital decided to discharge him to the rehabilitation unit in Akka Hospital, the small PRCS hospital just across the road from Chatila. I took his older brother, Adham, in the NORWAC ambulance transferring him. Adham was a handsome, intelligent engineering student at the Arab University in Beirut. Polite and friendly, he was, as a devout Muslim, slightly embarrassed at being a passenger in an ambulance driven by a woman. Sitting beside me, he expressed ambivalence about the idea of single career-women and said he thought he would never find the right woman to marry. His father was dead so he was now the head of the family and, as he talked about Jihad, I understood why the family were so grateful to me. They believed that Jihad had received first-class treatment at AUH because I had accompanied him. He said that poor people were known to have been turned away from private hospitals or given third-class treatment if they could not pay. I still don't believe this to have been the case, but I never convinced them.

Trouble was brewing over the NORWAC clinic. One

faction in the camp wanted the building to be a nursery school, which it was before it was damaged in the first Camp War. Another group, politically opposed to the first, wanted it to remain as a clinic. Ben and Barbara had run a first-aid and dressing clinic in the 10-day clash in September. Dirk was now running a primary health-care clinic there and they did not want to lose these services. Tempers were hot and the two factions almost came to blows. Eventually it was agreed that the clinic would remain temporarily until a new building could be found to house it.

Ben, employed by the PRCS, had defended its role as a clinic and by so doing had got on the wrong side of Um Walid, who regarded him as a troublemaker. At one day's notice she transferred him to the camp at Rashidiye, south of Sour, the southernmost camp in Lebanon, saying that he would never set foot in Bourj al Barajneh again. I was terribly upset to see him go. He had become a good friend in the three weeks I had known him.

Around 15 January, fierce fighting broke out in East Beirut between rival Christian groups. At night, from the roof of the hospital, we looked across to East Beirut only 2–3 kilometres away. We could see the red flashes of bombs exploding and hear the blasts a few seconds later. Several buildings were on fire. 'Come and see film *Beirut*,' said one young man sitting in the shadows.

At the end of December a Syrian-sponsored peace agreement for Lebanon, the Tripartite accord, had been signed in Damascus by Walid Jumblatt for the PSP, Nabih Berri for Amal and Elie Hobeika for the Christian Lebanese forces. But the Christian President, Amin Gemayel, had refused to ratify it. By 16 January, Hobeika's forces were defeated by those of Samir Geagea, who was also opposed to the agreement. Hobeika and his supporters were thrown out of East Beirut, leaving hundreds of Christians dead in the streets.

44

A few days later, Adham came to tell me that Jihad was at home. He had grown depressed in Akka and had insisted that his family take him home. There were two French physiotherapists working in Haifa Hospital and I took one of them, Dominique, to see Jihad. He was smiling and happy at home, the movement in his right leg had improved and there was a flicker of movement in his right hand. Dominique promised to visit him for regular physiotherapy and showed Adham how to help Jihad exercise.

I was persuaded to stay for a bite to eat, which turned out to be a huge meal. The house was small; there were only two rooms for the mother and five children but, as usual with all the houses in the camp, it was kept spotlessly clean. The family were friendly and warm but formal customs were observed as a mark of respect. It is not customary for an unmarried man to sit next to an unmarried girl, unless they are intended or engaged, so I was left sitting alone on one sofa while the rest of the family sat on the edge of Jihad's bed and on the other sofa.

As January wore on, the tension around Chatila increased alarmingly, and there were sporadic clashes between the inhabitants and the Amal militia outside. One afternoon, Lieve and I took a service taxi to the camp. At the Amal checkpoint just outside the perimeter we were stopped by a young militiaman, who looked about 15 years old, with heavy-duty lace-up boots and a skinhead haircut. He demanded that the driver show his papers, then told him to get out so he could search the car. The driver objected and shouted that he had better things to do than waste all his time at checkpoints being searched for no reason. The young man, his authority threatened, took two steps backwards, shouting and slamming his Kalashnikov into its firing position. Lieve, next to me in the back, drew a sharp breath and tried to shelter on the floor. I stared into the eyes of the young man with the gun. I couldn't believe this was happening. I was afraid, but really the situation seemed completely unreal. At last, the taxi-driver grudgingly consented, got out of the car and the young militiaman stepped forward to search the boot. He seemed satisfied and waved us on.

For several days at the end of January, there was heavy fighting around Chatila. Dirk was visiting Lieve when it began and did not come back to Bourj al Barajneh for a week. It was too dangerous for people to move in and out of Chatila most of that time. Several were injured and two killed. I thought often of Chris Giannou working in the operating-theatre without an anaesthetist.

In Bourj al Barajneh, people were tense, afraid that the fighting would extend to us. The children were kept away from their schools which were all outside the camp, in case anything happened while they were there and they could not return. There were no parks or playgrounds for the children so they played in the streets and in derelict houses. One evening around 6 p.m., the moment came that I had been dreading. Shooting broke out in the street that formed the camp's border at the bottom of the hill, the other end of Bourj al Barajneh from the hospital. Everyone was on 'Istanfar', red alert. It was the first time I had seen the Palestinians mobilise, ready to fight and defend the camp. Hurrying through the alleyways leading from the clinic to the hospital, I passed several groups of men carrying machine-guns, rifles and B7s (rocket-propelled grenades), and wearing jackets loaded with ammunition, cartridges and hand-grenades, going to take up position in buildings around the perimeter of the camp. Among them I recognised a local shopkeeper and the ice-cream seller. Off-duty staff were gathering at the hospital. The duty doctor was Dr Iklas. Dr Samer, who had recently qualified in Spain and lived with his family in the camp, was also there. He even looked like a Spaniard, with a little goatee beard. As we waited, I listened to the shooting in the distance. I felt increasingly anxious. At that moment, there was nothing we could do but wait but, expecting the worst, Dr Samer and I busied ourselves by counting the available empty beds in the hospital and deciding which of the patients we could possibly send home if there was a sudden influx of wounded.

After an hour and a half, the shooting stopped. No one had been wounded. The hospital staff drifted off home. 'Next time,' I thought, 'we may not be so lucky.'

As I passed my room, I looked in through the open door. A very old man, grey and balding, slightly overweight, and wearing Paisley flannelette pyjamas, was sitting on the sofa. He spoke to me in perfect, slightly old-fashioned English in a rather hurried, breathless voice.

'Please excuse me, I do hope I am not intruding. I have come here to shelter. My name is Arne Aout. I live in the house with the paraplegics but it's not at all safe, you see. If we could be given a house at the centre of the camp instead of at the edge, this would not be necessary. And I am not at all well. I have refractory anaemia and a very rare blood group. Do you think you could help me find some blood?'

'Has your anaemia been investigated?' I asked him.

'Oh yes,' he replied 'thoroughly investigated. 'I have all the papers in my room. Would you have the time to come and visit me? I could show them to you.'

I promised I would go as soon as I could.

The following afternoon after finishing in the hospital I went to visit Arne Aout in the house where he lived with six others, all of them paralysed paraplegics. He himself was not paralysed but because he was so old and frail and had no family in Lebanon he was looked after in this 'nursing home' run by the PRCS. The house was only 50 metres from the hospital but was indeed rather exposed near the edge of the camp on the side facing the airport road.

Arne Aout came out of his room, greeted me enthusiastically and produced the papers bearing the results of his investigations. I glanced through them and asked some questions about his health. The investigations had been thorough and showed no reason for his anaemia, but I knew that all anaemias have a cause and it is simply a matter of being able to find it. As most of his tests had been done some years before I thought it would be worthwhile repeating at least some of them.

The paraplegics, delighted at receiving a new visitor, gathered round the table in their wheelchairs and insisted that I stay to drink tea and then coffee.

'Where did you learn to speak such excellent English?' I asked Arne Aout.

'I studied philosophy at Oxford University in the 1930s,' he explained. 'I had a wonderful life until 1948. After University I went back to my home in Jerusalem but I left in 1948 because of the war.'

'Have you never been back?' I asked.

'Only once,' he replied 'For years I was not allowed to, but in 1984 I was given permission to visit my family. My visa ran out after a month but I wanted to stay with my family. I am over 80 and I wanted to end my life in my home town. I applied to the Israeli authorities, but they would not extend my visa for a single day. Will you be able to help me find some blood for another transfusion?'

'First we should repeat your blood count and do a few investigations,' I told him. 'Come to the hospital in the next few days.'

Barbara's friend Mohammed, who had gone off to the Gulf to work, had a younger sister called Souhar. Two days after the outbreak of fighting she came to the clinic. She was distraught. In tears, she told us that her father had gone shopping the day before in Hamra, the main shopping street in the city. He had not returned home. No one had seen him. Barbara and I went to comfort Souhar's mother, Um Mohammed, who was desperately anxious but thought that he might have stayed with relations or friends outside the camp because of the fighting around Chatila. We discussed

48

going to look for him, but because it was still red alert in the camp, everyone advised us not to go out. By the next day he had still not returned and a delegation of women went to look for him. They toured the hospitals and found him in the morgue at the American University Hospital, riddled with bullets.

They story which emerged was that, during the fighting around Chatila, an Amal militiaman had been killed. Furious, some other Amal men set up a checkpoint nearby. In one of the cars which they stopped was Souhar's father. When they saw his Palestinian identity card, they pulled him from the car and shot him at the roadside. Several other Palestinian bodies were laid out in the AUH morgue. They had been found dumped in a cemetery near Chatila.

The women came back and told Um Mohammed what they had seen. Someone came round to tell us. Barbara and I hurried through the narrow, muddy streets to Souhar's house where about 20 women were crying and wailing. All we could do was administer some Valium to Souhar, who was sobbing and throwing herself around hysterically. Poor little Feraz, her six-year-old brother who was mentally handicapped from a condition called craniostenosis, in which the skull does not grow properly and prevents normal growth of the brain, was frightened and confused. He kept trying to comfort his sister. We too were upset and angry, having known and liked the man. He was a kind, gentle man who had never picked up a gun.

Two days after the funeral, Barbara and I visited again to give our condolences. We sat drinking the traditional unsweetened bitter coffee, served in small china cups without handles, from a large ornate brass coffee-pot heated on coals. Feraz had been told that his father was dead, but I don't know how much he really understood. He ran about merrily, greeting people, oblivious to the solemnity of the occasion. There was a photo of the father on the wall; next to it was a photo of his other son, killed in the first Camp

War. Most houses in the camp had photos on the wall of family members who had died in the violence in Lebanon.

I was coming to the end of my three-month stay in Lebanon. Should I volunteer for another three months? Chris Giannou urged me to stay because there was still no other qualified surgeon for Bourj al Barajneh. Haifa Hospital was improving. We were seeing more patients and carrying out more operations, but progress was agonisingly slow. On the other hand, my three months in the Lebanon had gone by so quickly I felt I had achieved very little. I could now speak some Arabic but otherwise I was only just beginning to get the hang of everything. When I shared these feelings with Sol-Britt she said, 'Don't worry, things will get better.' She, too, wanted me to stay. Hassan, the theatre nurse, told me that the people of the camp wanted me to come back. They felt reassured knowing a surgeon was in the camp.

I remembered the night when there was fighting on the front street, and thought what it could have been like with no surgeon in the hospital. I thought of some of the things I had achieved, of Suzanne who could now wear shoes, of Omar who was walking again. I thought of those long conversations in my room with the lonely Dr Iklas. I thought of everything there was to do – of patients awaiting skin-grafts and plastic surgery, of the struggle to organise the hospital so that it could provide a better service. . . . I decided, if MAP agreed, to come back.

At the end of February, Barbara and I went home to England. After debriefing by Rafiq, the director of MAP, I asked if he would consider my going back for a second term. He laughed and said, 'Yes,' but first I should rest and allow the strain to wear off.

I did manage to relax. It was an extraordinary relief to be in a peaceful country without the sound of gunfire or the threat of war, but all the while I had the feeling that I was wasting time. In the comfort and quiet of my parents' home in Maidenhead, I broached the subject of my going back to the Lebanon. They were no more keen than before the first visit, but they had seen me go and come back unscathed and, as I told them more about the work out there, they agreed that it was of value.

I enjoyed the comforts I had missed and which we take for granted – fresh milk delivered to the door (there was only powdered milk in the Lebanon), hot water from a tap, windows which closed properly and were not broken, central heating – and I visited many of my friends in England. When I told one of them about my work with the Palestinians, she said, 'But what about the massacres of innocent people carried out by the Palestinians?' She mentioned the attacks carried out by the Abu Nidal group at Rome and Vienna airports that January.

I didn't have a good answer. I also condemned and detested such acts of violence and thought they served only to set back the Palestinians' real cause.

In the MAP office one afternoon I met Susan Wighton, a red-haired Scottish woman in her early twenties. She was short like me, but lively, attractive, confident and knew a lot about the Palestinians. A fully trained nurse, and more importantly a specialist in primary health care, she had applied to work in the camps. We in MAP thought she would be ideal to take over from Lieve and Dirk when they left in September and Susie reluctantly agreed to wait until then.

Chapter 4

A week later I was back in Beirut, loaded down with surgical instruments, medicines and books for Haifa. The books were for the doctors who were starved of postgraduate education. A reference library is a vital tool in a hospital, and the ongoing medical education is reflected in better care for the patients. With the books to guide us, I hoped to initiate more discussions about interesting cases. Perhaps the doctors would start thinking about how to improve services in Haifa instead of belly-aching about their lot.

Some people in the hospital were surprised to see me. They hoped that I had gone for good, out of the way of their power games. But most were welcoming and the hospital staff came rushing out of their rooms, crowding round me to shake my hand. I think they were surprised, too, amazed that anyone who knew how hard and dangerous life was in the camps could possibly want to come back.

The political situation was much calmer than before. There were reports of intermittent fighting around Chatila, and Chris Giannou was being kept busy but, apart from a few sporadic clashes, Bourj al Barajneh was quiet.

The weather was sunny and warm. I spent a pleasant weekend in Sour with Sol-Britt and the new Swedish team. On Saturday afternoon, Sol-Britt and I drove into the Palestinian refugee camp of Rashidiye to collect Ben from the clinic where he was working. He seemed delighted to see us and put his arm around my shoulders and hugged me.

'It's rather isolated here and I get lonely,' he confessed. 'But it has its compensations.' He took us up on to the flat roof of the two-storey clinic to look around. Rashidiye camp is built on the coast, just south of Sour, virtually on the long silvery sandy beach, and is surrounded by fields of orange trees and vegetables. Many of the small white plaster houses have tiny gardens in which to grow vegetables or raise a few chickens. Looking south over this peaceful rural scene, the farthest headland visible was Ras Nakoura, about 15 kilometres away.

'Beyond that is Palestine, or Israel as it is now,' said Ben.

As we stood there, we heard a distant bang and a puff of smoke appeared about a kilometre away, followed by a second. Two rockets had exploded in the fields.

'They probably came from the so-called security zone where the Israeli Army continue to occupy a strip of Lebanon, or from northern Israel,' said Ben. 'There are exchanges of rocket fire every few days.'

In the flat in Bourj al Chemali I talked with Ben. He missed Bourj al Barajneh and wanted to hear all about it. I told him that we missed him too. People were always asking, 'Where's Ben? When will he come back to Bourj al Barajneh?' I missed Ben's companionship, his smile, his easy confidence with people, and his knowledge about the Lebanon.

A Palestinian friend working for the International Red Cross in Sour spent Saturday evening with us, and on the way back to the flat after dropping him off, Sol-Britt and I were stopped at an Amal checkpoint. Sol-Britt rolled down the window and put on her best smile. A youth of about 15 sauntered over and asked us where we were going. As Sol-Britt explained, I saw the young man reach into the pocket of his combat trousers. For a moment my heart stopped as he thrust his hand through the window of the ambulance. But in his hand was only a boiled sweet, which he gave to Sol-Britt. He then produced another for me, smiling shyly.

This checkpoint was a temporary one, unlike most which were in fixed positions. We knew a Palestinian who called checkpoints 'checkinpoints', which inevitably we further garbled to 'chicken points'. Temporary checkpoints like this one we called 'flying chicken points'.

The following day, Ben came with Sol-Britt and I back to Beirut. Ben did much of the driving. He had no Dutch driving licence but had applied for his Lebanese licence and was learning to drive. He recalled his first driving lesson in Beirut a few months before. 'I was going around the block for the third time with Wencke in the passenger seat,' he told us, 'when two gunmen jumped into the road and ordered us out of the ambulance. We protested but one prodded me in the chest with his gun, so we got out and they made off with the ambulance leaving us on the pavement!' Ben laughed at the memory. 'That was the end of my first lesson.'

In Saida, halfway between Sour and Beirut, we had a picnic of chicken, garlic sauce and pickle on the battlements of the old Crusader castle which juts out into the sea, and I persuaded a passer-by to take some 'holiday snaps' of us with my camera.

A week after my return, Lieve moved from Chatila to live and work in the clinic in Bourj al Barajneh. To ease the staffing shortage in Haifa and to forge closer links with the hospital, she and Dirk took on-call duties there in the afternoons. For me, this was a happy time. Lieve and Dirk were by now close friends and I enjoyed their company in the evenings in Haifa. It was wonderful not to be the only foreigner in the hospital.

On 1 April there was another clash at Chatila. Akka Hospital, just across the road from the camp, was stormed by Shiite women and men armed mainly with clubs, shouting, 'Kill them! Kill them! Burn the hospital!' With the help of Sheikh Kabalan, a prominent Shiite cleric living in a flat in the hospital, the few Lebanese soldiers guarding the hospital managed to turn the angry mob away, but many of the patients and staff left.

Haifa Hospital now had a new director, Dr Rede. A Palestinian in his early thirties, he had been born and brought up in Bourj al Barajneh and trained as a doctor in Romania, where he had met and married his wife Erica. A kind, sympathetic man, scrupulously honest, he had dark curly hair and wide-set eyes. He seemed trustworthy and efficient and I was pleased that he had come.

He and his wife had been living in a flat in Akka Hospital, where Erica worked, and he had been commuting the short distance to Haifa. After the attack on Akka they left their flat and came to live in Haifa.

Every evening now we spent discussing 'the situation'. Small shifts in the fragile balance of power in the Lebanon could spark off a battle that would ruin many lives. People were acutely aware of this and constantly discussed any political changes. Everyone had their own forecast for the next few days or weeks. Very few people tried to look more than a few weeks ahead because unpredictable events inside or outside Lebanon could suddenly alter the whole picture. It was like a kaleidoscope – one small twist and a completely new pattern appears.

We Westerners soon came to have exactly the same discussions, albeit most of us found the situation in the Lebanon nearly incomprehensible. With each new turn in events we tended to think, 'Oh well, it can't get worse'; then it got worse. But it also got worse for the Lebanese and Palestinians, the poor as usual suffering disproportionately, so our reasons for staying on to offer aid and relief became stronger.

As March turned into April, things started to get very much worse. First, there was a rash of kidnappings of foreigners. British teachers Philip Padfield and Leigh Douglas at the American University of Beirut, and an Irish teacher, were kidnapped. The students and staff at American University went on strike for a day and protested for their release, but to no avail.

For a few weeks Dirk had been travelling in a service taxi to and from Sour to keep the clinic in the local village going during a gap between doctors from Sweden. During this time his Lebanese fellow-passengers were surprised to see him still travelling and most were very protective of him. Total strangers would insist on paying his fare, would sit him in the middle in the back of the taxi, where his blond hair was less obvious, and if stopped at checkpoints would tell the militiamen immediately that he was a doctor. Lieve was always tense when she knew he was travelling until he sent a message saying he had arrived.

Despite Dirk's reluctance to leave the clinic in the South unattended for a few weeks, when the kidnappings started we decided that it was too risky and that Dirk should stay put in Bourj.

Sol-Britt was still moving around when necessary, but devised a system whereby she telephoned the Norwegian Embassy to give exact details of her whereabouts.

The second bad moment came on Tuesday, 15 April 1986, when we heard on the BBC World Service news that in the early hours of that morning the US Air Force had bombed Tripoli, the capital of Libya. The US accused Colonel Ghadafy of acts of terrorism and after his public denials they decided to teach him a lesson. Margaret Thatcher's Conservative government gave permission for the American F1-11 bombers to take off from bases in Britain. They bombed a mixture of military and civilian targets, including Ghadafy's residence, wounding two of his children and killing his four-year-old adopted daughter. The raid produced outrage in the Arab world, and even Palestinians who had told me that Ghadafy was mad thought that the American raid was a shameful and heinous crime.

There were immediate repercussions in Lebanon. The following day the two British teachers and an American librarian were murdered by their captors and their bodies dumped in the Chouf Mountains. A British cameraman, despite having an armed Lebanese escort, was kidnapped on the airport road as he was leaving the country. The climate for foreigners, especially British and Americans, in West Beirut suddenly became very hostile. Western journalists were evacuated from West Beirut to East Beirut by helicopter, and on Thursday 17 April the World Service made a special announcement to British subjects in West Beirut, telling them to stay indoors and to telephone the embassy for instructions. There was no telephone in the camp, so that was out of the question. Lieve, Dirk, Sol-Britt and I discussed the situation. There was no possibility of kidnappers entering the camp to take us, and Palestinian friends advised us not to go beyond the perimeter. Many came to reassure us of our continued safety in the camp. We decided to stay put.

On Saturday 19 April, 35 British people were taken from a meeting place in West Beirut to East Beirut with a heavily armed escort. Even if I had wanted to go with them, which I didn't, to get to the meeting place in the city I would either have had to pass through the southern suburbs where many of the hostages were probably held, or brave the airport road. It was much safer to stay in the camp. One young man with an old leg-wound, who hopped around the hospital on crutches, offered to take his machine-gun and fight off anyone who tried to take me. Rashid, a hospital employee, brought me a box of strawberries to cheer me up. Adham, the brother of Jihad, came, concerned about my safety. He also told me, 'Don't leave the camp. Our house is your house. Please come and stay at any time and if you need anything my mother or my family will provide it.' Watching television that evening I saw protests and demonstrations in Britain against the US air-raid and I was heartened that I was not alone in my feelings. Lieve, Dirk and I were now in the position of many of the young men in Bourj al Barajneh, confined to the camp for the foreseeable future. Someone teased me that I was now worth one million dollars on the international hostage market, a joke I didn't find very funny. It was no great hardship staying in the camp. We were able to buy food and most things we needed from the small shops inside the perimeter.

Women had not yet been kidnapped. Arab battle philosophy granted them a sort of unwritten immunity and Sol-Britt was able to visit us escorted by a Lebanese driver. She brought news that Chatila was peaceful, a buffer force installed around the camp after a peace agreement in Damascus between Amal, PSP and pro-Syrian Palestinian groups. But that was the only cheering news during those days. The grim repercussions of the kidnappings, and bombing of Libya, continued. The *Daily Star*, the excellent English-language weekly newspaper, on which we depended for much of our information about the situation in Lebanon, ceased publication when the British editor, Robin Mannock, decided to leave West Beirut. Then it was announced that Alec Collett, a British employee of UNRWA who had been kidnapped, had been killed. His captors released a ghoulish video of his so-called 'execution'. Lieve and I were visiting Hassan's family on the evening of 24 April, when the video was shown on the Lebanese television news. To eerie, melancholic background music a hooded figure was shown being hanged from a tree in a garden full of flowers. The victim twitched a bit, then became still, swinging gently round. I felt sick and angry. It was a macabre display of the most vile, perverted brutality. A dispute was going on as to whether or not the victim was actually Alec Collett. He had apparently lost a finger in an accident; the victim shown seemed to have all 10 digits. But to me the argument was irrelevant. Even if it wasn't Alec Collett, then some other poor anonymous sod had been hanged for nothing.

As we sat there watching this gruesome show, mortar fire was being exchanged across the Green Line from east and west. Some of the bombs were being launched from Shiite positions near the camp. It was a warm evening and from the open door of Hassan's house we saw the red streak and heard the whoosh as a rocket flew low over the house and then the bang as it exploded some 80–100 metres away. Lieve and I jumped up, ready to dash back down to the hospital, but Hassan said he thought the rocket had fallen well outside the camp. But after a few minutes we heard shouting and running and people yelling that it had exploded in the camp. We ran back to the hospital, getting there just as the first of the wounded was carried in. It was a young girl seriously wounded in the head. Then another arrived – a man with severe shrapnel wounds in his arm, legs and chest. And then a woman was brought in dead, wrapped in a blanket. She had been almost decapitated. The girl with the head injury was transferred in a PRCS car to a neurosurgery unit while we patched up the man.

I did not have a chance to look at the dead woman, as I was dealing with one of the other casualties, but Lieve did. It was Nidal, our hospital administrator. Poor Nidal. Her life had been one tragedy after another. In 1978 her husband disappeared during the Israeli invasion of South Lebanon. Nidal spent years looking for him before resigning herself to the fact that he was dead. She carried on working for PRCS, but sent her children to Jordan to live with relatives. Twice she had lost her house, destroyed in the fighting. Her life had been threatened and she had narrowly missed being injured a few weeks before. The latest blow had been when her brother was arrested south of Beirut by the Syrians. The day she died she was visiting friends for a cup of tea when the rocket hit their house. It was not intended for the camp, and officials in East Beirut later sent condolences.

Nidal's death was a major blow. There was no one with her experience and energy to replace her in Haifa. There were three days of mourning in the hospital, which we all attended. After the burial, 50 chairs were set out on the first-floor landing. We all filed in and sat down in silence to drink the traditional bitter coffee. On the third day, at midday, we attended a funeral meal in a house near the hospital. Um Walid attended all the ceremonies and I got to know her a little better. Despite her autocratic ways, I liked her and admired her courage. Ignoring a number of threats on her life, she had stayed in Lebanon after the Israeli invasion in 1982 to run the PRCS.

The vision of the twitching man swinging around by a rope round his neck wouldn't leave my mind. It was so cold-blooded and cruel. The kidnappers had denounced the men they had killed as CIA agents. I did not believe it for one minute and nor did anyone else. The awful irony was that the hostages, like most people who stayed on in West Beirut despite the risks, were sympathisers, recognising the hardship of the poorer Muslim communities and entirely innocent of any surreptitious dealings.

Chapter 5

Despite the horrors of the previous few weeks, I remember that the weeks at the end of April and the beginning of May were pleasant, relaxing times. The Lebanese summer had begun. Every day, there were cloudless sunny skies and the temperature was usually in the 70s. We had grown accustomed to not being able to leave the camp and, in the late afternoon after work, Lieve, Dirk and I would sit on the small balcony of the clinic, looking out over the ramshackle buildings sprawling up the hillside and listening to the sounds of constant building repair work, the squawking of chickens, and the slow plaintive strains of the call to prayer from the loudspeakers of the two mosques. As we drank our tea we would talk about the rewards and difficulties of working in the camps and share our bewilderment at each daily encounter with the paradoxes of the Lebanon. On the roofs of other buildings, in the orange light of the sinking sun, young men and boys exercised their homing pigeons. It was a peaceful scene and sometimes I almost forgot the ever-present threat of war.

Lieve and Dirk had come to the Lebanon out of political conviction to show solidarity with the Palestinian cause. They were committed members of the Labour Party in Belgium, which sent medical teams to various parts of the world to work with people involved in a struggle for liberation. But, now that they were here, they saw the importance of specialised medical work and wished they had had more training in primary health care before they came.

I thought they were doing a magnificent job. They had managed to set up two primary health-care clinics, one in

Chatila and one in Bourj al Barajneh, and Dirk had done a survey of the vaccination status of Lebanese children in the South.

He found that it was worse than in most Third World countries. Less than 10 per cent of the children had been properly vaccinated. In 1981 a survey had concluded that to organise a primary health-care programme in the southern suburbs of Beirut was 'virtually impossible', and yet that is exactly what Lieve and Dirk were doing.

My motivation had been different. I had come to the Lebanon for humanitarian reasons, wanting simply to work as a doctor. But now that I was here, having witnessed with my own eyes the misery caused by the gross injustices done to the Palestinians, I had developed a strong sympathy for their cause. But I still wanted to keep out of politics – it's a dirty game, I thought, and nothing I had seen in the Lebanon had changed that view.

When we were not on the balcony, we spent our free time making visits in the camp. We were overwhelmed with invitations to visit friends and local families. If we had accepted them all we would have spent all day every day visiting, drinking tea and coffee, and eating. Luckily, many invitations and social engagements are rather loose in the Arab world. People agree a time, then turn up late or not at all and many arrangements are made '*inshallah*', which literally means 'God willing', but is used to mean: 'Maybe I'll come, but maybe not.' '*Bookera inshallah*' ('Tomorrow, God willing') is sufficiently vague to mean 'maybe never' and is the Arabic equivalent of '*mañana*', but even more indefinite.

One regular visit I did make was to see Jihad. His brother, Adham, would lead me through the narrow twisting alleys to their house, as I still couldn't find the way on my own. Jihad was walking with a stick and some movement had returned to his right hand, but he was still clumsy and he talked very slowly. His family were amused, because although I had difficulty following what they were saying I could understand his slowly pronounced speech perfectly.

Morale in the hospital was improving. The books I had brought from London were being read avidly by the doctors, the hospital was filling up, the new wards on the first floor were open. Specialists were visiting for consultation and teaching, and, hearing that the treatment was very good, patients were coming to the hospital from outside the camp. Their numbers increased after Dr Mounir brought a Sri Lankan woman to Haifa from Akka Hospital. A gynaecologist there had procrastinated for days, debating her diagnosis. Dr Mounir was convinced that she had an ectopic pregnancy and after seeing her I completely agreed. A woman who may be in early pregnancy, with abdominal pain, collapse and sudden profound anaemia, has an ectopic pregnancy until proved otherwise and a delay in operating can be catastrophic. Together we operated and took out the ectopic pregnancy. She made an excellent recovery and left, singing the praises of Haifa Hospital.

The presence of Dr Rede and his wife Erica living in the hospital also did much to raise morale. Dr Rede was unselfish and fair, and he asked nothing for himself. Life in the hospital must have been quite hard for the Redes. They had little privacy and Dr Rede was constantly being called upon to solve some petty problem. But they never complained and for me their presence was a great boost. Not least because if I stayed in the hospital, I had good company in the evening.

Their friend Abu Taisir often came to the hospital and the three of them taught me Arab card-games. Abu Taisir was a middle-aged man with greying hair, one of the 'wise men' of the camp, who gave advice to the committees and help to the hospital patients and their families. He was also a long-time patient of Dr Rede, having once been peppered with hundreds of pieces of shrapnel in the buttocks and thighs. He came to Dr Rede regularly for the troublesome, painful pieces to be taken out.

Bourj al Barajneh was governed by a committee made up of 'wise men' like Abu Taisir, most of them elderly men who would have been the village chiefs in Palestine, and the leaders of the various political groups, who were also in charge of the military organisation of the camp. The committee was responsible for policing and the administration of justice, for planning of building works and repairs, for appointments to positions of authority, and for defence. As far as I could tell, its members were elected by an informal collective decision. They met regularly in the houses of the committee members or in one of the mosques. Sometimes the meetings were public.

The political groups consisted of all the various Palestinian factions, some owing allegiance to Arafat's PLO, others, like the Popular Front for the Liberation of Palestine (PFLP) and Abu Moussa, opposed to Arafat and allied to Syria, and still others, like the DFLP, who were broadly neutral. In Bourj al Barajneh they generally managed to submerge their differences and unite against the common enemy outside.

The effect of being cooped up in the camp all the time created stress in the young men and tempers occasionally flared. One such young man was 'Ringo'. He was a good-looking, curly-haired, generally amiable young man who wore incredibly tight jeans. He lived in his family's house just behind my room in the hospital. One day he had an argument with his cousin just outside the hospital and they both pulled out their guns and started shooting. The noise in the hospital was deafening. I was working with a nurse called Amal (namesake of the militia) who, terrified at the sound of shooting at such close range, starting sobbing hysterically. She crouched on the floor in the corridor with her arms over her head and started praying. I sat with my arm around her, trembling myself, until the shooting stopped. Much of it had apparently been into the air but the camp police were called and both men spent several days under arrest in 'prison' somewhere in the camp.

A few days later, I saw Ringo from my window. He grinned sheepishly and waved. Later that evening, when I returned to my room, the window was open and a single red rose was lying on the bed.

There were many weddings at that time. It was almost a year since the first Camp War and the period of mourning was almost over for families who had suffered bereavement, so now the weddings could be arranged. Several times we were invited and when the sister of Hassan, the hospital nurse, was to be married, Lieve, Dirk and I accepted.

The wedding was held on the roof of the bridegroom's house. Fifty or so chairs were set out but were soon filled and guests spilled over on to the roof next door. The concrete roof was a sun-trap and after an hour Hassan's friends tried to fix up some shade for the sweltering bride and groom with a bedspread. She was in a white satin and lace crinoline dress, heavily made up, and he wore a smart dark suit. The bride and groom began the dancing and were followed by guests who danced in turn in twos or threes. The girls loved to dress up in a colourful, flamboyant, modern Western fashions, and dance with a kaffiyeh, a chequered Palestinian scarf, tied around their hips. They danced wildly to traditional Arabic music played live by a group consisting of Ali the bongo drummer, a guitar player, and a singer, Hassan's cousin. The Arab music was interrupted for 20 minutes by another cousin, an eleven-year-old who brought his own modern post-punk tape so he and his two friends could show off their breakdancing and robot dancing.

Pineapple juice and delicious coconut biscuits were passed around and, because this was a Muslim wedding, there was almost no alcohol. It didn't seem to make much difference.

65

Ten older women in long dresses and scarves, Hassan's mother and her neighbours, got carried away dancing the 'Debke' – a dance in which the dancers link arms in lines, and involving some fancy footwork and much jumping, stamping and shouting. One of the women grabbed the bongo drums from Ali and the others pulled Lieve and I up to join them. Although we got terribly mixed up with the footwork (I trod on Lieve more than she trod on me), we managed some good stamping and jumping before, sweating from the hot sun, we collapsed into our chairs. The older women went on dancing. 'I'll be seeing some of them tomorrow,' I thought, having already treated two of them for arthritic knees.

These happy days could not last and, towards the middle of May, a new series of events took place which made the people in the camp uneasy and nervous. Three young Palestinians, one of them a cousin of Hassan, and a Lebanese, ventured out of the camp one day and went swimming in the sea. When they came out of the sea they were 'arrested' by Amal militiamen, taken to one of the militia's interrogation centres and beaten and tortured for two days before being released. They went straight to Mar Elias camp, a small Palestinian Christian camp near the sports stadium. It is a safer part of Beirut than Bourj al Barajneh because it is in an area controlled by the Druze. From there the three Palestinians were brought to Haifa Hospital, where we dressed their wounds and rehydrated them with drips.

They were not very seriously hurt but were covered in bruises, had lost the skin off their knees and shoulders, and their wrists were swollen as a result of being tied up and dragged around the floor. Their bodies also bore the marks of cigarette burns and weals from being whipped with electricity cables. The boys were dehydrated because they had not been given any water but had been made to drink their own urine. It was the first time I'd treated the victims

66

of torture and I felt revulsion and anger at such degrading brutality.

Amnesty International had asked me to provide documentation about any illegal imprisonment or torture I encountered and the men consented to be photographed provided their faces were not shown.

Soon after, Ali, another young man employed by the PRCS as a driver, was taken by the Amal militia. He was beaten, especially on the soles of his feet and hands, and kicked in the groin. Luckily, when I examined him, I found he had no broken bones but, because of the swelling and the pain of the bruises, the visiting orthopaedic consultant advised padded plaster of Paris splints for rest.

After his discharge from hospital a few days later, Ali recovered his health and his courage. He sent a message via Hassan that he wanted to see me. The next afternoon Hassan and I left the hospital and, after a couple of minutes' walk, entered a small courtyard through a wrought-iron gate. Ali's pregnant young wife met us at the door and led us inside. Ali was lying in bed while his baby played on the floor beside him. He had a strange story to tell.

After his initial beating, he had been thrown into a cellar. In the cellar was a very old French man. Ali gathered that the old man had been kidnapped in the city three weeks earlier and although he had been ill-treated at first, he was now left alone in the cellar. The old man was very kind to Ali; he cleaned his wounds and gave him his own trousers because Ali's were filthy; he also gave him his blanket to sleep on. After two days, Ali was taken out and dumped in the street. At first he had been too frightened to talk at all, and he was still very anxious, convinced that if his captors knew he had passed on information, they would catch him again and kill him. But because the old man had been so kind, Ali wanted to help him in some way. He decided to tell me, on condition that I would not reveal the source of my information. I asked Ali if he knew where he and the

Frenchman had been held and he described a building only about half a kilometre away from the camp on the airport road.

Back in the clinic, I told Lieve and Dirk the story and we worked out that the old man was probably Camil Sonntag, an elderly Frenchman who had disappeared a month before. It was still considered unsafe for us to leave the camp, so I called Mar Elias on the hospital walkie-talkie radio and left a message for Sol-Britt that we wanted to speak to her. A few days later, she visited us and we told her the story. It was going to be hard for her to get a message to the French authorities. Most of the foreign embassies in West Beirut were closed and many diplomats and journalists had left Lebanon altogether, but Sol-Britt said she would do all she could. The house Ali described was in a Shiite neighbourhood, and we thought the building was controlled by Amal. But we knew that hostages were likely to change hands, sometimes being kidnapped by one gang, then sold and passed on to their eventual captors. So it was most likely that the old man would already have been moved. Alas, Sol-Britt was able to do very little as the French Embassy was closed and she was unable to cross the Green Line.

The spate of kidnappings stopped as suddenly as it had begun and Ben came to visit twice, travelling into Beirut from Saida, where he was now working. We still thought it was rather dangerous and I accused him of overworking his guardian angel. He had been given a partial reprieve by Um Walid and was working in a new PRCS hospital in Ain al Helweh, a large Palestinian camp in Saida, a bit nearer Beirut. But he still wanted to come back to work in Bourj al Barajneh.

During these two visits I became very close to Ben. We sat up talking until late into the night, after Ben's many visitors had left and Lieve and Dirk had gone to bed. On his second visit Ben had brought me a copy of *A Farewell to*

Arms by Ernest Hemingway. It is a powerful novel about Hemingway's experiences as an ambulance driver in Italy in the First World War and his passionate romance with a British nurse.

During the week of 19–26 May, tension increased sharply around Bourj el Barajneh. Sniping began and a few grenades exploded in the camp. Several people were wounded by shrapnel, and two young men and a girl were shot walking at the edge of the camp. One of our nurses was shot in the leg as she left the camp at 8 a.m. after night duty, and on Saturday the 14th, a nine-year-old boy was killed by a sniper, shot through the chest. 'Where is your camera now?' cried one of the nurses. Lieve ran to fetch hers and photographed the dead child. There were other worrying signs; Amal were erecting large piles of sand 50 metres away from the edge of the camp. People in the camp became increasingly uneasy and agitated.

Ben, Lieve, Dirk and myself all slept in my room in the hospital in case anyone was injured. Again Ben and I sat up late with glasses of hot milk, talking softly until well after Dirk and Lieve were asleep.

'I want to be here in Bourj al Barajneh with you,' Ben told me. He promised to ask Um Walid to reconsider her decision not to allow him to work in Bourj.

Before he went back to Saida the following morning, Ben left me a letter in which he spoke of how much he had enjoyed his visits to me and that he thought he was falling in love with me. I was overjoyed, because I too was falling in love with him.

Ramadan, the Muslim month of fasting, had begun on 9 May. The previous year, the attack on the camps began at the beginning of Ramadan and people feared it would happen again. About three-quarters of the camp population were observing the fast, eating and drinking nothing between sunrise at about 4 a.m. and sunset at about 7.30 p.m.

At around 6 p.m. people became restless after the whole day without eating, drinking or smoking. Work in the hospital was supposed to continue normally, but it was very hard on those who were fasting and we tried not to overwork them. The first two weeks of Ramadan had been peaceful but, because of the increased tension, two doctors instead of one were put on duty every night. I saw some families leaving the camp, all their belongings packed into old cars.

There was a feeling of panic about these people, but curiously, I did not feel worried at all. Ignorance is bliss and I did not really believe a big fight would happen again. I thought that the Camp War had been fought and finished with a year ago.

In that same week, Ben came to visit again on an evening when there was heavy east–west fighting. Ben, Dirk and Dr Samer went up with Hassan on to the roof of the hospital. Just as they got up to the top a huge rocket exploded just outside the camp, not 100 metres away. Dirk at once came back down the stairs, looking ghostly white, followed by Dr Samer, running. 'I learned only one thing up there,' he said, 'how to run down again very quickly.' Hassan, more accustomed to such things, came down with Ben, saying excitedly, 'Wow, the shrapnel reached all the way to here!' I was glad I had been cowardly and hadn't gone with them.

For most of the day on Sunday 25 May, we could hear sporadic gunfire around the perimeter of the camp, and the occasional crash of a bomb exploding. The streets and alleys were deserted. People were staying indoors. About 20 of them, mostly women and children but including two old men, came into the hospital with blankets and I saw a man armed to the teeth arrive with his family, carrying his new baby. They came to shelter in the hospital either because their house was flimsy with only one floor and would not withstand a direct hit, or because they lived at the perimeter of the camp. The five-storey hospital was a much safer place and the people simply spread out their blankets in the corridors or slept on the storeroom floor. They brought food, blankets and small Primus stoves.

That Sunday morning, Dr Rede and Erica left Bourj al Barajneh to visit friends. They did not return to the camp that evening.

Chapter Six

On Monday 26 May, shouting and screaming in the emergency room and the sound of machine-gun fire around the edges of the camp woke me up at 5.30 a.m. I tugged on trousers and a T-shirt over my pyjamas, grabbed my white coat and ran down to the emergency room, meeting on the stairs Dirk and Dr Maher, the duty doctors.

Four young men lay in the emergency room. All had been shot. The camp was under attack. A fierce battle was raging outside with bombs dropping every few minutes. The young men who carried the stretchers were still crowding around their wounded friends, comforting them and getting in our way.

We had only one small operating-theatre, one anaesthetist and one anaesthetic machine, so could only do one operation at a time. We began immediately. The first was a 35-year-old man with a chest and abdominal wound. We put in a chest drain to drain out the blood and then operated on his abdomen. I struggled to control the profuse bleeding from his shattered liver and kidney. He needed rapid blood transfusion.

A nurse brought in a message that the laboratory technician could not find enough blood from donors of the right blood group, so I gave instructions for the blood collecting in the bottle from his chest wound to be used. It was still not enough. Just as we got the bleeding under control, after taking out his kidney, he died.

I felt momentarily all in, but we still had two more major cases to do. I went out to the emergency room where Dirk and Dr Samer and Salah, the head nurse, were looking after the other two, who were stable. There was just time to gulp down an energising glass of sweet Arab tea before they wheeled the second patient into the operating-theatre.

He also had a bullet wound in the abdomen. Dr Maher, the junior surgeon, would perform the operation while I assisted, ready to take over if there was anything complicated. Thank God it was simple – only a few holes in the small bowel – and we were finished in an hour and a half.

The third was a good-looking man called Abul Feda. I explored his upper arm wound which confirmed a fractured humerus, a severed artery and vein and an injury to major nerves. I repaired the artery and vein, approximated the nerves, thoroughly cleaned the wound and applied a plaster of Paris slab.

Even inside the operating-theatre in the basement we could hear the muffled intermittent bursts of gunfire and an occasional explosion.

It was about 2.40 in the afternoon before we finished and we were just sitting down for a cup of tea when a nurse came to tell us that more wounded men had been brought in. Two of them were seriously hurt. Dr Maher and I found one young man in the X-ray room with wounds in both sides of his chest and also his abdomen. His name was Fadi. Dr Samer had put in chest tubes, but his breathing was still frantic as he thirsted for air.

'It's hopeless,' muttered Dr Maher to me as we went to look at the other badly wounded man in the emergency room. He was worse, his breathing had stopped and was only kept going by a tube and a ventilating bag which Dirk was squeezing.

I had to make an agonising decision and make it immediately. Both were close to death. I might, perhaps, be able to save one of them. We took Fadi, the one with the chest wounds. He had the better chance of survival as he was still breathing on his own.

His operation was long and complicated. We had to take out his spleen and one of his kidneys, then stitch up a small hole in the aorta and repair more small holes in the bowel and a tear in his diaphragm. The operation took more than six hours. His heart stopped twice on the operating table and we had to massage it to start it. He needed 10 pints of blood, more than the total amount of blood in his body, but he survived. The other man died.

At about 10 p.m. Dr Maher sat down in the ante-room of the operating-theatre for a welcome glass of tea, a cigarette and something to eat. I was so tired I was well past feeling hungry. We had been operating continuously for over 13 hours. It was my first experience of complicated bullet and shrapnel wounds but there had been no time for doubts. I had just had to get on with it. Dr Maher had been a real help. He had seen many more of these injuries than I had.

Salah, the head nurse, came in to tell us all was quiet at last. He had cleared out a stock-room next to the X-ray room for the post-op patients. It was a good place, in the safety of the basement and near the operating-theatre and emergency facilities. We would also be able to keep a close eye on them.

When Dr Maher had finished his meal we went out to check the patients. I asked Salah if he could make up a 'cut-down' set for putting up drips in a hurry. 'Yes,' he said, 'but first I'm going to pray,' and he disappeared into the pharmacy at the end of the corridor, which they were using as the prayer room. In the circumstances, praying seemed quite reasonable.

The boy with the arm wound, Abul Feda, was calling, 'My arm hurts, my arm hurts.' I felt his pulse to check the repaired artery. It was good. I gave the nurses instructions to give him an injection for pain.

The other two patients were all right. Fadi was still alive, which was more than we had hoped for. He had been so close to death. I looked at him anxiously, lying in the makeshift ward. There were many potential complications in the forthcoming days.

At last I climbed wearily up the stairs from the basement. I stepped past the two old men who were sleeping in the stair-well on the half-landing, and noticed that the number of people sheltering in the hospital had swelled to about 50. Despite the relative calm now, they showed no sign of going home.

Dirk and Lieve were in my room and welcomed me with a cup of tea. Lieve had been down in the clinic all day, setting it up as a first-aid room, but she had seen only two minor wounds. When she heard from Dirk the difficulties he, Dr Maher, Dr Samer and I had had coping with the number of wounded in the hospital, Lieve felt she would be more effective working here. Couldn't a nurse run the first-aid clinic?

Dirk was deeply disturbed by the death of Khalid, the other badly wounded man, who had died while we operated on Fadi. Dirk had known him and he felt he had not done enough to save him. When the two men came to the hospital, Dirk had given Fadi the only oxygen line because of his chest wound. 'You want me to die,' Khalid had gasped in English. He collapsed within minutes and died soon after and although Dirk accepted that Khalid was almost certainly not savable, he was inconsolable.

I slept well, despite the noisy coming and going in the hospital, and the next morning I hungrily consumed a breakfast of tea, bread and cheese. Then I made a ward round and I was relieved to see Fadi awake, struggling for life, his chest improved. In Europe, after such an operation, Fadi would be screened by a whole gamut of biochemical tests on his blood and urine, but here in Haifa the only test available was a crude blood-count. The other four seriously wounded men were also making good progress. This was largely due to the work of Amal, the wonderful nurse who was the namesake of the militia. She was clever, highly

trained and hardworking and no longer seemed in-
capacitated or immobilised by fear as I had seen her before.
'I feel quite well down here in the basement,' she said. 'I'm
busy and that helps.'

Then the shooting started again. By late morning the
battles around the camp were fierce and furious and soon
more wounded arrived at the hospital. First, two minor
injuries, then a one-year-old child shot in the head (his
mother had been wounded by shrapnel) and a fourteen-
year-old girl, the sister of one of the nurses, shot through
both eyes. Both needed highly specialised units, so the hospital administrator summoned the Palestinian military
chiefs who contacted the Amal commanders on the walkie-
talkie and begged them to let us transfer the girl and the
baby. They consented and one of the hospital administrators
agreed to drive them out in a car. The baby's mother went
with them. Soon after they left, more wounded were brought
in and we were back in the operating-theatre.

In the afternoon, we were resting in my room when there
was a knock on the door. It opened and in walked Dr Rede
and Erica. I was so relieved to see them I hugged them
both. Throughout all the turmoil of the last 36 hours they
were often on my mind. Were they safe? Would they ever
be able to get back in?

'We came in with the driver,' explained Dr Rede. 'We
told the men at the checkpoint we had gone out with the
girl and the baby and they let us in.'

Erica was still shaking with fear, so Dr Rede told us what
had happened.

'On Sunday afternoon, when we drove back towards the
camp, the roads were blocked by Amal militiamen and we
dared not approach. We went back again to our friends
and stayed the night there. Yesterday we tried again. We
drove around the camp, but bullets were flying everywhere.
It was impossible to enter.'

He had not slept for worrying about us and could not rid

himself of guilt at being stuck outside away from his people just when they needed him most. He and Erica had risked their lives coming in.

Now we were six doctors in the hospital and Erica was an experienced midwife.

Our rest was shortlived. The fighting flared up again and more wounded arrived. We operated through the night until six the following morning. I slept for a few hours, then was woken by a voice saying, 'Come quickly, there's a wounded man!'

The man was fat and middle-aged. He had an appalling gunshot wound in his abdomen. I knew it was an M-16 wound. An M-16 is a high-velocity rifle made in the USA. The bullet travels extremely fast and causes a cavitation effect, a sort of shock wave as it passes through the body, so that although the entry wound is very small, 0.5cm. in diameter, and the exit wound not much bigger, it causes enormous damage inside.

When we operated on this man, the worst damage was to the liver and kidney, and there were holes in the bowel. But all the organs looked bruised and swollen, as if they had been taken out, stamped on and put back in. The man's name was Abu Raif. He survived the operation, but remained critical.

By the end of these three days, I was exhausted and completely disoriented. Day and night were indistinguishable. I could hardly remember which patients we had operated on by day and which at night. We had slept when we could. I had not had time to eat properly and had smoked too many cigarettes. We had received more than 50 wounded, many of them serious, and 4 dead. We could not be sure that these four were the only dead not knowing the fate of those transferred outside the camp.

Salah, the head nurse, cleared out another stock-room to accommodate the overspill of critical patients. The first room, only 4 metres square, now contained five patients recovering from major, complicated operations; there was only just enough room to squeeze between them. We sarcastically named this room the Intensive Care Unit, although the only resemblance it bore to a European ICU was its sick patients. It was poorly lit by one bare bulb in the middle of the room. One of the three small windows was broken and boarded up with plywood. Grey paint was peeling off the walls. There was just one dirty sink in one corner with cold water only. In another corner stood a small nurse's desk, one leg supported on bricks, adorned not with electronic tracers and bleeping gadgetry, but with a pair of scissors for the nurses to cut up gauze for sterilisation. Each patient was cluttered with tubes and drips with the bags hanging down from nails banged into the walls.

The eight nurses on duty were struggling desperately to look after so many seriously ill patients. There was only one qualified nurse on duty during each 12-hour shift in both the basement and on the first-floor wards, where 20 or so not-so-serious patients were cared for. Both a help and a hindrance to the staff were the families of the wounded, who brought linen and extra food and helped to wash the patients. Most of the wounded men had large families who lived in the camp only a few minutes away from the hospital. They all wanted to come and help and often got in the way of the nurses. Mothers, wives, aunts and sisters would come and sleep under or between the beds amongst the chest-tube bottles and catheters. We put a stop to this when one of them accidentally disconnected a chest-tube bottle when she turned over in her sleep. After that we made a rule of only one relative to a bed, but it was a constant battle to uphold it.

Over the next few days, Fadi determinedly inched his way towards recovery, against my expectations. The others in that room were also doing extremely well. But Abu Raif, victim of the M-16 rifle, developed complications. He was a well-educated man who spoke good English and was always cheery, never complaining. It wrung my heart to watch him deteriorating daily. Eventually, as a result of the stress of his injury, he vomited a torrent of blood which we could not control and died shortly afterwards. I was left with a feeling of sadness and defeat and, although the surgery textbook stated plainly that 'high-velocity bullet injuries of the liver are almost universally fatal', it did not make any difference.

Although the three surgeons, Dr Rede, Dr Maher and I, discussed the patients, and how best to deal with their complications, there were no back-up laboratory or X-ray facilities and no comforting umbrella of senior specialist colleagues from whom to seek advice. Often I felt very alone.

The fighting continued over the next two days, but it was not so fiercely intense and although the wounded continued to arrive, it was only at the rate of about 10 a day. People were staying indoors in the underground shelters. At last we were able to draw breath and to spend time organising ourselves.

Dirk and Lieve stayed in the hospital all the time now, sharing my room. Lieve's first-aid clinic was run by nurses in shifts. During the fighting, the camp population of children, adults and old people still suffered from the normal gamut of coughs, colds and abscesses. So Lieve and Dirk organised daily out-patient clinics. By now there were 50 post-operative out-patients needing regular dressing changes and they also attended Lieve and Dirk's clinics. For the emergency room operations and care of the critically injured, we divided ourselves into three teams, one surgeon and one other doctor to work on one patient as far as possible. Dr Samer, the junior orthopaedic doctor, would look after the daily care of the orthopaedic patients while we surgeons concentrated on the surgical cases.

On Saturday 31 May, I woke up with a jolt at 5 a.m. It was still dark. Bombs were exploding all around every few seconds. A deafening crash thundered above me, delivering a whack in the chest, like a body blow, as the shock wave hit the hospital. The whole building shuddered and I could hear the sounds of smashing glass, of bricks and rubble falling. 'Oh God,' I thought, 'the whole hospital is falling down!' I scrambled out of bed and dashed out into the corridor with Lieve and Dirk. A large shell had made a direct hit on the hospital. It was followed closely by a second and a third.

People came crowding into the corridor from their rooms. Children were crying. Nurses were helping those who could walk down the stairs from the first floor above us. Up there people were screaming.

Khaled, a young hospital administrator, whose main occupation, I thought, was maintaining the crease in his immaculately pressed trousers and smiling and joking with girls, charged blindly up the stairs into the billowing dust and smoke. He pushed between a nurse and an old man recovering from pneumonia, severing the drip connection, and with other young men close behind him, began rescuing bedridden patients, carrying them down the stairs in their beds, as bombs shook the building every few seconds. It was an extraordinary demonstration of selfless courage.

A seriously wounded man, upstairs because our 'Intensive Care Unit' was full, was hurriedly put down in the corridor, chest tube, drips, bags and all, amongst the feet of the sheltering people. His colostomy bag had come adrift and I got down on my knees on the floor and tried to clean him up, set right all his tubes and make him comfortable.

Astonishingly, no one was injured in the hospital. A boy with a broken leg told me excitedly how a tank shell had come in through the window of his ward, shot past the feet of his and another boy's beds, gone out of the door, across the corridor, through another room housing an old lady, and buried itself in the far wall without exploding.

The blanket bombardment went on for three hours with bombs exploding everywhere in the camp every few seconds.

The noise was deafening. Initially, I went downstairs towards the emergency room but Samir, the radiographer, guided me to the safety of a corridor behind the emergency room saying that the brick outside wall of the emergency room was not enough protection from these shells. We lived through the shelling out in the crowded corridor, dashing into the emergency room to attend to the wounded, then retiring again to the safety of the corridor.

Extraordinarily, there were only five or so casualties during that whole three hours and they all had only minor wounds. I think it was because the bombing started so early in the morning and most people were asleep in the shelters or in their homes. Once it started, it was suicidal to venture outside anywhere. But it was still amazing, as whole houses of flimsy breeze-blocks and plaster could be completely demolished by a direct hit in such an attack.

The ordeal of the bombardment was lightened by a constant supply of sweet black Arab tea. By now I had grown to like it very much and I found it calmed my nerves. The Arabs drink at least as much tea as the British, which was great for a tea addict like me. The right time for tea was all the time.

Of course we now knew that tanks were stationed around the camp. As the shelling went on, one of the male nurses explained the different types of bombs to me. Tank shells travel in virtually a straight line when they leave the muzzle, so they hit the first obstacle in their path. Only the top floors of the hospital were exposed to these because the basement, ground floor and part of the first floor were shielded by surrounding houses. Rockets, which were the ones coming in threes and fours, were launched from the backs of trucks and fly in a slight arc. But the mortars fly up high and then drop, almost vertically, at the end of their flight, like the trajectory of a ball thrown over a high fence; these could drop into the narrow alleys and streets, exploding on impact. Bigger mortars could blow down walls but the smaller ones were only really dangerous to people caught outside.

Just after 8 a.m., the bombing died down and we drifted upstairs from the basement to the doctors' room, the room opposite mine. There was a brief breakfast and then we made our daily ward round. Abul Feda was still complaining, 'Oh, doctor, my arm hurts!' but now smiling with it. Fadi was doggedly optimistic as always, now with fewer tubes but still with a number yet to go. The others seemed to be speeding back to health. As so often I was amazed at the resilience of the human body.

We decided it was too dangerous to put patients back up on the first floor, so two other rooms on the ground floor next to mine were converted into wards and all the offices squeezed into one small one.

Once again our respite was brief. The bombing began again. A man was brought in dead, almost decapitated, and put straight into the fridge. Another had a high-velocity bullet injury of his thigh; the bullet had removed a large chunk of bone and severed the blood-vessels, so we operated to repair the vessels. Then a man was brought in with shrapnel in his chest. I took him to the room adjacent to the emergency room to put in a chest drain and was just preparing him on a low bed under the window when there was the flash and a huge bang just outside the window. Rubble and dust rained in on us. I dragged myself to my feet, checked that neither of us was wounded and calmly moved him to a bed away from the window. There had been no time to be frightened or to react in any way. It was all over before I understood what was happening and, because of that, was less frightening than I had imagined being very close to a bomb would be.

The bombing continued on and off for another week. The wards filled up and overflowed with patients. We opened up a room for them in the basement of the other wing of the hospital, but it was not well ventilated and a long way from the emergency areas, so we tried to put only convalescent patients down there. There were not enough beds and three patients had to sleep on the large physiotherapy floor-mat which measured about two metres square. Despite the assistance of numerous volunteers who came to the hospital to do what they could to help us, the nurses were stretched to the limit.

We often had to drag the patients into the safety of the corridors, including two young men with broken thighs, who were confined completely to bed on home-made traction apparatus. They remained cheerful throughout. The heavier the bombardment, the more they laughed and joked, keeping people's spirits up. Once one of them called me over to look at his knees shaking in mock fear and I giggled. I found that a serious situation often produced incongruous results, and I often giggled during the shelling out of sheer nervousness. Dr Maher had a different reaction. He would go to sleep.

The two boys with fractured femurs spent several nights in the corridor, one behind the other against the wall, singing duets late into the night. An irascible old man in another bed sometimes lost his temper, shouting, 'Shut up! Can no one be allowed to sleep around here?'

I now slept well despite all the noise, but bombing close by still woke me up. Lieve could sleep through anything, even a bomb landing on the hospital. One morning she wrote in her diary, 'Quiet night, slept well,' then looked at Dirk's diary, which said, 'Heavy bombardment at 3.00 a.m.'

Lieve, Dirk and I became very close during these weeks. We did not leave the confines of the hospital at all. In the evenings, whenever possible, we sat in our room to talk about patients and problems, or in the doctors' room where an old television was set up and we could watch the half-hour news in English at 6.00 p.m. and, incongruously, World Cup football from Mexico. Thair and his friend

Ahmed came to visit us in our room, bringing us news from the front lines, which they said were holding steady.

On one side of the camp, the fighting was from building to building across a narrow street about 10 metres wide, with the Palestinians and Amal shooting at each other from close range. When the fighting started, the houses on the edge of the camp were swiftly evacuated and taken over by the fighters. On the other three sides of the camp, the battle took place over stretches of waste ground, at longer range. Amal tanks were stationed around the camp behind buildings or huge piles of sand, moving forward to fire on the camp and then retreating out of sight. The Palestinians would shoot at them with rocket-propelled grenades during the few seconds they were in view. Thair and Ahmed told us that during the intense bombing on Saturday morning, 1,500 bombs fell on the camp in three hours. They also brought us things we needed. When the small stove, on which I made tea, ran out of gas, Ahmed came to the rescue with a little electric cooker from home.

The month of Ramadan ended on 8 June but the fighting continued. On 10 June, six men were killed in two bomb explosions. I knew of course that Amal militiamen were being injured and killed as well, and we could sometimes hear the sirens of the ambulances taking their wounded to hospitals. 'What a stupid war,' I thought. 'All this killing for these small camps full of refugees.' But so much of the Lebanese civil war has been fought like this. Battles were waged and men died fighting for control of small districts, or single streets, sometimes even for one strategic building. And, as usual, those orchestrating the war were nowhere near the front lines.

On the morning of Wednesday 11 June, after more than three weeks of fighting, a ceasefire was declared, enabling the burial of the six dead from the day before. By the fridges to the side of the entrance hall of the hospital, the bodies were washed. Sixty to seventy women crowded in the entrance hall, singing, chanting and wailing their grief, and waving scarves. Two fainted with emotion and had to be revived. Erica and I stood amongst the women pushing up the stairs. I felt rather uncomfortable, as if I was intruding on a private ceremony, but friends came and stood with us and Erica explained that it was not an intrusion. To attend was to respect the dead. Later, at about 11.30 a.m., a message reached the hospital via the walkie-talkie that an Iranian delegation, accompanied by Hezbollah (Party of God) soldiers and maybe 10 ambulances were entering the camp, having successfully negotiated with the Amal militia to be allowed to evacuate the wounded. Dr Rede thought it was prudent for Lieve, Dirk and I to stay out of sight, not because there was any direct danger to us in the camp, but because of the dangers of kidnapping outside the camp. It was probably better if we kept a low profile, he explained, as they did not know all the credentials of the Muslim fundamentalist soldiers accompanying the delegation and did not want us to be recognised on some other occasion outside Bourj al Barajneh. Rather disappointed, we waited in our room.

First, the Iranian delegation went on foot to inspect the mosque and saw that it had indeed been hit by shellfire. Then they came to the hospital and began to take out the wounded, starting with those in the shelter for convalescent patients. But, after about 10 minutes, shells began falling around the hospital. The evacuation broke up in chaos and the Iranians left the camp in haste. They took with them an old woman recovering from pneumonia, another old woman who had had a hip replacement before the war, the nurse shot in the leg at the start and two men not wounded in the war. Fadi, who was still desperately ill, was left behind. Ktaeb (Christian) Radio and the BBC announced the successful evacuation of wounded. I wrote in my diary, 'They took three women and two men. Then Amal started to bomb the hospital and fire into the camp, so the Iranians left in a hurry. They did not take the one really sick one who desperately needed to go out for further investigations. *Damn it.*'

Lieve and Dirk and I sat together that evening and we talked over the events of the day. Then the talk turned to another, more personal matter. They had noticed that I repeatedly read the letter from Ben, usually just before I went to sleep. Deducing the truth, they offered to teach me some Dutch. They were Flemish-speaking Belgians and Flemish is very close to Dutch.

'Well, we had better start with some romantic Dutch,' said Dirk. 'Let's begin with "I miss you".'

I giggled and wrote it in the back of my diary under the heading 'Lessons in romantic Dutch'.

Chapter 7

Still the fighting went on. We were operating nearly every day, sometimes for most of the day. We tried to save cases that seemed hopeless, partly through naivety and partly because occasionally we had an unexpected triumph when a wounded man survived despite our predictions. I later heard that this was a great boost to the morale of the camp. The people of Bourj al Barajneh did not expect miracles from Haifa Hospital but they trusted us to do our utmost for our patients.

By now the psychological pressure of weeks of bombardment was beginning to tell on the population. Patients came to the clinic with psychosomatic complaints, aches and pains, or occasionally to the emergency room in a state of hysterical collapse. The nurses were affected too, complaining of pain in the head, in the whole body and dizziness. The standard treatment for this, prescribed by the Palestinian doctors or occasionally administered by a more senior nurse, was a drip infusion of a litre of dextrose, usually with some vitamins added, to run over a couple of hours.

At first, I was critical of this treatment because it has very little, if any, scientific basis and you might as well administer two or three cups of sweet tea. But I stopped criticising because it worked. These nurses were suffering from physical and nervous exhaustion and lying down for two hours with a drip confirmed their exhaustion, attracted sympathy and care, and allowed them a complete rest. More often than not, they were able to return to normal work immediately after the 'infusion' was over. We doctors were also exhausted; only Dr Samer seemed never to tire.

We still had to retire to the corridors on occasion when

the shelling was heavy. One day, Erica grabbed my hand and pulled me out of the doctors' room as three rockets hit the side of the hospital. I thought the doctors' room, being on the ground floor, was not exposed, but one evening a shell smashed through the wall near the ceiling. Luckily, no one was in the room at the time and the rubble and shrapnel were soon cleared away.

The only times I saw Erica really frightened were when she heard the sonic boom as Israeli planes flew over, breaking the sound barrier. Then she would pale and begin to shake. She had been in West Beirut during the Israeli air-raids in 1982. 'Those bombs were quite different,' she said. 'Just one could demolish a whole apartment block.'

I admired Erica. She was a strong woman who had given up her life in Romania to come with Dr Rede to work in the Lebanon and support him and his people during this crisis. She spoke only French and Arabic, and our conversations were mainly in French with a few Arabic words thrown in when my O-level French let me down.

Even a ceasefire agreement signed in Damascus by PSP, Amal and the pro-Syrian Palestinian groups on 15 June did not stop the fighting. On the afternoon of 17 June, a fifteen-year-old boy was brought in, shot through the abdomen from the back. Small coils of intestine protruded from the wound. It was a typical high-velocity bullet injury, so, knowing that the operation would be lengthy, I ran to my room to visit the toilet before I started. I was surprised to see Ahmed, our friend from the clinic, lying on the couch. He looked terribly upset. 'What's the trouble?' I asked. 'Are you ill?'

'No,' he replied, 'but please look after that wounded boy. He's my brother.'

'Of course I will,' I said, but I did not voice my fears about it being a high-velocity wound.

The operation on Ahmed's brother, Tarek, took two and a half hours. The bowel was badly damaged and we had to remove about two feet. There was also much bruising and severe bleeding from the blood-vessels supplying the bowel, but, miraculously, very little other damage.

That evening I wrote in my diary, 'It seems this war is by no means finished.'

On Saturday 21 June, there were intermittent attacks all day. Many bombs were hitting the hospital. Prolonged bombardment all around the building could be very intimidating. A claustrophobic, gloomy mood of pessimism would grip everyone inside. That evening we were again forced to shelter in the corridors and even the fractured femur duo were subdued. Then suddenly I heard several big explosions in the distance. The bombardment of the camps ceased immediately. There was a moment of silence, then people started clapping. The boys with the fractured femurs cheered.

'What's happening?' I asked.

'That's bombing from the mountains,' said Hussein. Walid Jumblatt's PSP had allowed the Palestinians to shell the Amal positions from the Chouf Mountains overlooking West Beirut, to relieve the pressure.

The silence was glorious. It felt as if a weight had been lifted from us and we enjoyed an elated, peaceful evening. That night I slept very deeply.

Sunday and Monday remained fairly quiet and we were at last allowed to transfer Fadi and another very sick old man. I felt very emotional saying farewell to Fadi. As he was carried out on a stretcher, Fadi grabbed my hand and kissed it, forgetting his dreadful outbreak of herpes cold sores, and said, 'Goodbye, my sister.' 'Goodbye, Fadi,' I said in Arabic. 'Get better soon.' I never saw him again. Four weeks later I heard that he died from further complications.

The news on the radio that night said the peace plan was being implemented and a 'buffer force' of PSP, the Lebanese Army and Syrian observers being moved in, but they were very slow in coming. A week after the agreement was signed, I wrote in my diary: 'No sign of buffer force here. However, Chatila is now peaceful and the buffer force installed there has stopped the fighting.' Eventually, the buffer force arrived at Bourj al Barajneh on Tuesday 24 June.

The next day, we got a surprise visitor from outside. Dr Diek, one of the orthopaedic consultants who used to come to the camp, managed to get permission to come in. We welcomed him warmly, kissing him on both cheeks. It had not been easy to get in. He had argued with the militiamen at the entrance of the camp for half an hour, when they tried to confiscate his papers. We took him to see all the orthopaedic patients. We had stabilised their fractures with plaster of Paris and traction, but some needed metal pinning. He selected a few to operate on.

Despite the presence of the buffer force, there was still sporadic sniping into the camp, and Dr Diek was nervous. He kept asking, 'Are we safe here? Is this room safe?' Then a delight. He handed me a letter from Ben. I stuffed it in my pocket and escaped at the first opportunity to my room to read it. Ben was in Beirut, staying at the NORWAC flat. He'd been there for two weeks, working in Mar Elias, carrying patients and equipment for the PRCS in the NORWAC ambulance because all their ambulances had been confiscated. His feelings for me were not changed and he couldn't wait to see Lieve, Dirk and I. I read the letter again that night before sleeping. At last I had a new letter to send me to sleep. For the past five weeks I had been reading and rereading a letter he'd sent me before the fighting.

The next day, Thursday, was quiet and Dr Diek was able to operate on several patients, assisted by the enthusiastic Dr Samer, who had managed the patients brilliantly in his absence. There were no cases of bone infection.

On Friday morning, I was in the shelter, changing the dressing of a woman who was recovering from an abdominal operation when Lieve came to tell me that Ben was on the walkie-talkie. I was so afraid that I would cry if I tried to speak to him that I made excuses and asked her to send him my love.

The next day, he managed to get through again. This time I steeled my nerves and spoke to him. It was such a relief to hear him. I spoke to him in Dutch, the only words I knew, telling him I loved him and missed him. Dirk was laughing. He told me that my pronunciation was so hopeless that Ben would never understand me.

Half an hour later fighting broke out again when the buffer force tried to make the Amal militia demolish their sand-hills. Several of the buffer force were injured and at 3 p.m. a sudden bombardment of the camps caught people outside in the streets.

Within minutes there were nine seriously wounded in the emergency room. It was mayhem. There were wounded men on the couches, on the floor, in the entrance, blood everywhere. Relatives and friends were screaming, refusing to leave their wounded loved ones. Three died immediately. Then a tenth came in. I could see he was seriously wounded in the chest, abdomen, arms and legs. There was nowhere to put him, so the stretcher-bearers took him to a ward. I left the other six doctors with the six who were alive and ran after him, checked him over, resuscitated him and sent him down to the X-ray room with orders to take him straight afterwards to the operating-theatre. Then I dashed back to the emergency room. One more had died. Two needed operations at once. The rest had multiple shrapnel wounds that could be dealt with in the emergency room when we finished operating. When at last it was all over, poor Dr Diek was badly shaken. 'It was terrible, so terrible,' he kept muttering.

By Sunday 29 June, real peace seemed to have arrived. There had been no casualties for two days. At midday I was sitting in the sunshine in my room, drinking tea after the morning round, when Rashid knocked on the door and opened it. 'Ben is in the camp,' he shouted excitedly. 'I don't believe it,' I said. 'It's true, it's true,' said Rashid and rushed off. I ran after him down to the emergency room to see Ben surrounded by a crowd of smiling people shaking his hand and hugging him. He looked so fit and well compared to the rest of us. We were pallid creatures, after so long indoors. I took his hand and gradually extricated him from the throng; then I led him to my room where we hugged and hugged. Dirk and Lieve came rushing in and embraced Ben. 'How did you manage to get in?' I asked. No one other than Dr Diek had been allowed in.

'I told them my wife was working in Haifa Hospital,' he said, 'and that I hadn't seen her for two months and did not know whether she was alive or dead. They felt sorry for me and let me in. But they made me leave the ambulance at the entrance and walk into the camp.' That meant crossing 50 metres of open ground exposed to sniper fire.

He told us news from outside, including what had happened to the first patients evacuated by the Iranians. 'They were hijacked by Hezbollah,' he said. 'They were first taken to Beirut Hospital [in a PSP area]. Then a group of armed men rushed into Beirut Hospital and bundled them out at gunpoint. In fact they weren't harmed but hijacked a few streets to Turk Hospital. It seems the director of Turk Hospital had a relative in Hezbollah and wanted the money from the PRCS for treating them.'

'Only in Beirut,' I thought as I listened, shocked and amused, 'could patients be kidnapped by a hospital.'

Ben went on: 'Turk Hospital did not have all the necessary high-tech equipment, so representatives from there visited Um Walid to ask her for one million lire to buy new equipment for the hospital. She told them she didn't have a million lire and they should let the patients go.'

Ben was still in the middle of his story when someone came to tell him that negotiations had been made with the

Lebanese Army to allow the transfer of wounded. He brought in the ambulance and, with two other cars from the camp, they loaded six patients, this time the most serious first, and took them to Akka Hospital. We asked Ben to try to come back with some medicines, which were desperately needed. He arrived back an hour later. The delivery of the patients had been uneventful, but an Amal militiaman had seen Ben putting bottles of medicine in his bag outside Akka Hospital and demanded that he give them up, threatening and abusing him and pulling his hair. Luckily, he had already secreted a few bottles inside the ambulance and they were not found. They loaded another six patients to take out and promised to come back the next day.

'Do you have to go out again?' I asked Ben as he was preparing to leave. 'Suppose the fighting begins again?' I was suddenly terrified that we would be separated again.

'It's OK now,' he said. 'There is a real peace.'

He was right. They came back the next day, were able to transfer some more patients and then stay in the camp. In the evening Hassan invited us to his home and we sat on the little terrace under the fig tree breathing in the fresh air and enjoying the warm night. It was bliss after having been cooped up in the hospital for weeks.

Ben stayed with Lieve, Dirk and I in our room in the hospital that night. We sat up drinking hot milk and talking about the last few weeks. Ben said he had on several occasions approached the Lebanese soldiers outside the camp, asking them to let him in, but had always been turned away. He thought they granted entry because he pestered them so much. Inevitably, the talk turned to the political situation. Ben said that there seemed to be no real political solution even though the Syrians had brought about 500 observers to West Beirut and the camps to keep the peace. The bitterness between Amal and the Palestinians was now so deep that further warfare seemed almost inevitable.

The next day, two Palestinian doctors were allowed in to

93

relieve us, so at last we had a day of rest. We couldn't relax until we had been down to inspect the clinic, which had been abandoned after a shell had landed at the top of the stairway, blowing out two walls and a door. There were heaps of rubble and stones and splintered wood and all the windows were broken, but the building was reasonably intact. We found the tail of the bomb lying in the wreckage. Thair and Ahmed and little Feraz came to help us clear up the mess and it was in good order by the evening.

Chapter 8

The ceasefire held and peace returned to the camp. UNRWA trucks with food supplies were admitted and the International Red Cross evacuated 45 patients. The people of Bourj al Barajneh picked up the threads of their lives and sounds of hammering and clanging started again in the early morning and lasted all day as people repaired their shattered homes.

We too had to do repairs. Ben fixed the shrapnel holes in the water tank on the roof of the clinic with rubber gloves, wood and chewing gum! Darwish, the local plumber, installed some new pipes and we soon had running water.

Children ventured out to school again, some more enthusiastically than others. Feraz, the six-year-old handicapped boy, often ran away from school and went home or came round to see us. He was fascinated by photographs and keys and, if we did not watch him closely, things would disappear and we would have to retrieve them from his secret box at home.

Lieve and Dirk began again organising a community health campaign and clinic, and we gave first-aid classes to several groups of young men and women. UNRWA were able to bring in spraying equipment and disinfectant to clean out the underground shelters and the rubbish dumps. Babies and children were brought in for general health checks and overdue vaccinations and in the hospital we revived the old system of clinics and operating lists and even started on some skin-grafting and reconstructive surgery. Patients who had been evacuated drifted back into the camp, complaining that staff in the hospitals outside did not care about them and they felt better in Haifa. My belief that they would receive better care in the other hospitals equipped with everything we lacked in Haifa was apparently not always reality.

When the ceasefire had held for two weeks, Ben, Lieve, Dirk and I decided to venture out of the camp. It was the first time I had been out for four months and I felt both apprehensive and elated. We drove in the NORWAC ambulance to Akka, about a mile and a half from the camp. My anxiety dissolved as I looked out at the bustling streets and people going untroubled about their daily business. In Akka Hospital we discussed with Um Walid how to find a new building for the clinic, as the group who ran the nursery school were again putting pressure on us to let them have it back.

Then we drove round to the entrance of Chatila camp, parked the ambulance and approached the Lebanese Army and Syrian checkpoint on foot. The soldiers thoroughly checked our bags and our NORWAC identity cards. As they were doing so, three men in plain clothes sidled over and began to talk to us. They said they were Syrian journalists. We chatted briefly to them, them walked into Chatila. We headed for the centre where the clinic was.

Wenke, a Norwegian nurse, and Regine, a French nurse, were upstairs in their new flat, two rooms opposite the old staff quarters. Within two minutes of our greeting them the Syrian 'journalists' appeared at the door with Dr Maher. They had followed us to the clinic and wanted to interview us about our work. Had we been in Bourj during the fighting? they asked. How was it? They were very polite but somehow they didn't seem like journalists. They behaved much more like security service agents, taking close-up pictures of the four of us individually, front and side view like police 'mug shots'. They asked us each our opinion of Hafcz al Asad, the Syrian President. 'Well,' said Ben diplomatically, 'he is always smiling on television.' Lieve snorted indignantly.

Dr Maher laughed after they had gone away, agreeing that their pretence of being journalists was not very convincing. 'But you must always be polite and co-operate with them,' he warned. Dr Maher was in very good humour and unchanged apart from his new brand of cigarettes, extraordinarily cheap Syrian ones which fell apart if you tapped them too hard. He was planning a book about the foreign volunteers working in the camps and had decided to call it *Birds from the West*. I giggled and tried to explain that 'birds' did not only mean birds of peace, like doves, but in English could be a rather disrespectful slang word for women. The explanation was lost on him. He was undeterred.

After a brief talk with Chris Giannou, we left Chatila and went to the NORWAC flat. For the first time in weeks I was able to relax. It was wonderful to know that I wouldn't be called, that there was no one clamouring for attention. Just to be alone with Ben, with no one bothering us, was heaven. In the camp there was no solitude at all – someone was always watching you, wanting to talk to you. And best of all, I had a hot bath in the flat, my first in four months. What luxury! We cooked a meal of spaghetti, then I fell into bed and slept soundly.

The next morning we took a service taxi back to Bourj al Barajneh. The car stopped at the Lebanese Army checkpoint on the airport road, 60 metres from the camp. One of the soldiers recognised Ben from his previous attempts to get into the camp, smiled, and asked about his 'wife'. The Lebanese soldiers kept us there for 15 minutes, checking our papers, then talking on their walkie-talkies for authority to let us go on.

As we waited we became very uneasy. There we were, four blond Westerners standing very conspicuously by the side of a road that was notorious as a kidnap area. People in passing cars looked at us curiously. At last we got clearance and started walking the 50 metres towards the camp. About halfway, I glanced over my shoulder and saw that a car had stopped at the checkpoint. The Lebanese soldiers were looking at us.

'Oh, no,' I said to Ben. 'That car is interested in us.'

'Just keep walking,' he said. But the car, a metallic-green BMW, sped up and stopped just in front of us. Inside it were two young bearded men in T-shirts and jeans. One got out, stood in our path, opened the back door of the car and said menacingly in Arabic, 'Get in the car.'

'What do you want?' said Ben. Lieve, who was on the other side of the road, thought they were offering us a lift and gestured, 'No, thank you.'

'Get in the car,' the man said again.

'No,' said Dirk. 'What do you want us for? We are going to the camp where we work. Our papers are in order.'

'Do you speak English?' I asked, smiling, trying to be calm though my knees were shaking.

'No,' said the man. Then he reached into the car, pulled out a Kalashnikov machine-gun and pointed it at us. 'I will take you to the office.'

We still pretended we didn't understand. I thought if we tried to walk on he might start shooting, so I said to him, 'We will go back to the soldiers. They will explain what you want.'

We walked back towards the five Lebanese soldiers at the checkpoint, who had simply stood there all this time, watching. I was aware that people were also watching from the camp. The car followed us to the checkpoint. Lieve and I sat down between two soldiers, determined not to budge.

'Where is the Syrian observer?' Dirk was shouting. 'Call the Syrians,' he said to the soldier with the walkie-talkie.

'Maybe you should just go with them,' said another soldier, who belonged to the Shiite 6th Brigade of the Lebanese Army.

'Why?' we asked. 'Who are they? Our papers are in order.'

Ben was talking to the man who claimed not to speak

English. It turned out that he did, in fact, speak it well, and in a last attempt to get us to go with them he repeated his demands in English. We stubbornly stood our ground. What could they do? They could not shoot us and risk shooting the Lebanese soldiers. And the soldiers were unlikely to stand by and allow them to manhandle us struggling into the car from their checkpoint.

After about 15 minutes of arguing, the two gunmen were forced to give up. They got into the BMW and sped off. As soon as their car was out of sight we scurried, almost running, into the safety of the camp. There we met Dr Rede, who had been informed that we were in trouble and was coming out to see what was happening.

We collapsed on to our beds and, over a much-needed cup of tea, decided that in future we must always leave and enter the camp by car. Those 15 minutes, spent standing openly on the airport road like that, exposed us to too much risk. As we calmed down, we started laughing. We regarded ourselves as among the lucky few who had escaped a kidnap attempt.

The wedding season returned to the camp. Life again became very pleasant and we were able to enjoy the long Lebanese summer of seemingly endless hot cloudless days. But I was overdue home. I had overstayed my three months by one and a half months. It was time to go back to England, to see my family, to report to MAP and, I hoped, to make preparations to return.

At the end of July, I returned home to England. MAP did not have an immediate replacement for me and, knowing there was still so much work to do, they agreed to send me back for another three months. I telephoned Susie Wighton, the Scottish nurse trained in primary health care. She was still keen to come and said she would resign her job and be available in two weeks. We began preparations for her briefing session and arrangements for her visa.

At the memorial service for Leigh Douglas and Philip Padfield, the two British hostages who were killed after the US raid on Libya, I met Terry Waite, the Archbishop of Canterbury's special envoy, and made arrangements to see him in his office in Lambeth Palace. There I told him what I knew about the old Frenchman, whom he agreed was probably Camil Sonntag. He said he would do what he could.

While I was in London I heard the sad news that Arne Aout, the man with anaemia, had had an uncontrolled haemorrhage from his stomach and died.

Chapter 9

Ben met me at Beirut airport in the blistering, relentless August heat. As soon as I stepped off the plane I felt again the familiar anxiety produced by the ever-present possibility of danger. I saw the familiar groups of armed men standing around on the tarmac and took part in the familiar argument with an immigration official about the validity of my visa. But despite all this I was happy to be back. Many people who have lived and worked in the Lebanon fall in love with the country and its people and I also was drawn back to it, attracted by the people, their warmth and hospitality and their resolute ability to ride the storms and carry on with their lives.

Even during the kidnappings earlier in the year, quite a number of Westerners had refused to leave, especially if their Lebanese friends provided a certain security. Now foreigners were drifting back into West Beirut. Lebanon is a country of extremes and, with the spate of kidnappings over, we were able to go on Sundays from the poverty and rubble of the camp to swim at the Sporting Club on the seafront in the fashionable Raouche district of West Beirut. Around the water, wealthy Beirutis sunned themselves in the latest bathing fashions. If they heard shooting, they would look up lazily to see if it was anything to do with them, or glance up resentfully at the distant dots made by the Israeli planes breaking the sound barrier on their 'reconnaisance missions'. The concrete jetties and stairways that jutted out into the sea from the rocky coastline were thronged with sunbathers, and waiters in white jackets bustled around behind the bar, serving drinks and food. The sea-water at this time of year was the temperature of a warm bath and its salty buoyancy meant you could spend hours effortlessly floating about in the sunshine.

The club was open to members and foreigners. One day we took Ahmed and Thair along, the only Palestinians in our party of foreigners. In the showers, Dirk had a conversation with a Frenchman, who remarked that it was wise to have brought along our 'bodyguards'. When he told us, we all laughed. Ahmed and Thair were far too interested in the scantily clad bathing beauties to guard anything. They disappeared for the whole afternoon, coming back once in a while to give us rapturous descriptions of yet another incredibly beautiful girl they had just been gawping at.

Soon after my return, Dr Rede's wife Erica went back to Romania, and Thair left for the Gulf. I was sad to see them go.

In early September, Susie Wighton arrived. She moved into the clinic with Ben, Dirk, Lieve and myself. Lieve began showing Susie the ropes, introducing her to people, visiting the nursery schools for health screening of the children and generally discussing the work. Lieve was very impressed by Susie.

'She is very knowledgeable and has good ideas about primary health care,' Lieve told me. 'It makes me feel much easier about leaving.'

Susie could already speak a few words of Arabic, having worked in the Gulf and visited the Israeli-occupied West Bank where she first developed a sympathy for the Palestinians. She was soon practising her Arabic, especially with the children who, curious as ever, crowded around her admiring her fancy ear-rings, many of which she generously gave away. About a week later, I was working in the basement of the hospital when someone came to tell me there was a physiotherapist upstairs to see me. I thought it was probably the Palestinian student physiotherapist with a patient for me to see. In the administrator's office I found a tall, thin, boyish man in his late twenties with short, straight, ginger hair. He was sitting between a large rucksack and a sausage-shaped holdall.

'Hello,' he said, holding out his hand. 'I'm Hannes, a physiotherapist.'

'Hello,' I said cautiously. 'I'm Pauline Cutting.' It came back to me that there had been some talk about an Austrian physiotherapist in the MAP offices.

'Welcome,' I said. 'This is a bit of a surprise. We didn't know you were coming.'

'MAP sent me,' said Hannes. 'But I went via Cairo where the Palestine Red Crescent Society made my travel arrangements.'

'Come with me,' I said. 'I'll show you where we live.'

Hannes settled in quickly. He was extremely amiable and – like Susie – could already speak some Arabic, having worked in the British Hospital in Nazareth. Hannes was a deeply religious Christian although he did not belong to any particular Church. 'You do not have to believe in any one church to believe in God,' he said. Each night before going to sleep he would read from the Bible.

Lieve and Dirk were coming to the end of their year's work in the Lebanon. The country was the most peaceful I had ever known it, so the four of us planned a short holiday trip before they left. In early September we set off into the Druze heartland of the Chouf Mountains south-east of Beirut, where the men still wear white skullcaps and black *cheroual* pantaloon trousers with yards of material belted in at the waist. Many of them were surprisingly fair with sandy hair and big bushy moustaches.

We stopped at the top of a hill and got out to look around. An old Druze man in traditional dress was walking up the hill, supporting himself on a gnarled stick. Ben asked him if he could take his photo.

'Of course you can,' he said, posing proudly. 'And please, come into my house here for coffee.'

We accompanied him in and met his son and daughter-in-law and their new baby. His wife was traditionally dressed in a long, heavily embroidered skirt, but was too shy to be photographed. Not so the old man. He insisted we took more photos of himself sitting upright on an old-fashioned sofa underneath pictures of his ancestors.

There are many colourful myths surrounding the Druze faith, but its origins are in Islam, from which it split in the eleventh century. The community remained closed and impenetrable, with strong clan and family loyalty. Walid Jumblatt, the present leader, comes from one of the most influential families and some Druze can trace family loyalty to the Jumblatts back for hundreds of years.

In the village of Beit-ed-din we met a group of Palestinians, some of whom had taken refuge from the Camp Wars in the Chouf, as the Druze were not hostile to them. We had come to Beit-ed-din to visit the palace of the Emir Bashir Chehab, the last Lebanese monarch, who died in 1850. The palace is well kept, its sand-coloured stone buildings and rose-gardens clean and neat. But it receives very few visitors now, and very few foreigners go there. One of the guards, who saw us wandering in the courtyard, came over with his bunch of keys and opened up the bathhouse with its pink marble rooms and bright mosaic floors and the small staterooms filled with paintings in rich, dark reds and golds, gleaming chandeliers and chairs cushioned in purple velvet.

Coasting down the inland side of the mountains we entered the southern end of the Bekaa valley plateau, a long wide fertile valley between the Lebanon and anteLebanon mountain ranges, with Mount Herman watching over it from the south. Syrian soldiers controlled the checkpoints and we could see their military trucks and encampments half dug into the ground every few miles.

The fields were full of tall green plants. I asked Ben what the crop was. 'It's marijuana, hashish,' he said. These fields of cultivated marijuana stretched out green and gold as far as I could see in all directions. With its high European street-value, it must have been a major cash-crop.

The town of Baalbek nestles in the foothills of the ante-Lebanon range at the north-east corner of the Bekaa valley and I could see, as we approached, the six remaining pillars of the Roman temple of Jupiter Heliopolitanus, or Baal, the semitic sun god. Baalbek is a very ancient town settled some time before 3000 BC. Legend has it that Adam lived nearby to the east and that Noah is buried in a sarcophagus at Krak Nooh, a village a few miles to the west. The town has seen countless battles, as invading armies from the north and south passed through the Bekaa valley. In modern times it has witnessed the battles of the Syrian and Israeli fighter planes fought in the skies.

Every telegraph pole in Baalbek bore a poster of either the Imam Musn Sadr, the religious leader of Amal, who disappeared in Libya in 1978, or Ayatollah Khomeini. On a hill, overlooking the town, stands the Sheikh Abdullah barracks which houses maybe 500 Iranian Revolutionary Guards and Hezbollah militiamen. There are rumours that foreign hostages were held within its walls.

We stayed that night in Baalbek in the PRCS clinic at the Palestinian camp of Wavell, sleeping on camp-beds in an empty ward. Ben knew some of the staff there and they gathered to greet us, crying out '*Ahlan wa sahlan*' or 'Welcome', and insisted on preparing tea and a meal of boiled eggs, bread, hummus and olives, which we ate at a low table in the tiny kitchen.

The next morning we visited the great temple complex, its entrance guarded by a Syrian tank which I was not allowed to photograph. The Romans built these magnificent temples to Baal (Jupiter Heliopolitanus), his son (Bacchus) and his daughter (Venus). They are grouped around the pre-existing Phoenician sanctuary and its sacred meteoric black stone. Many of the tall ornate Corinthian pillars and friezes of cupids, mermaids and dragons of the sea are well preserved and the temple of Bacchus is almost completely intact. Ben turned out to be a fount of knowledge about the history of the place, having studied classics at university.

Leaving Baalbek, we crossed the Bekaa valley westwards, passed nomadic bedouins in their black goat-hair tents, climbed up over the Mount Lebanon range and descended through the Cedars, the stronghold of the Christian Maronite community. We went north to the city of Tripoli in northern Lebanon (not to be confused with the capital of Libya). Ben had worked there in 1983 and, as we entered the Palestine Red Crescent Society hospital in the refugee camp of Bedawe, one of the cleaning women recognised him and he was immediately clasped in a bear-hug. Many people seemed to remember him. The following day as we were looking round the old city area, we sat down in a café, which Ben said had the best *kenaffeh*, a sort of pastry and cheese custard with honey sauce. It was delicious but, when we tried to pay, the waiter refused our money. 'It has already been paid for,' he said, pointing to a man who was leaving the café. In the doorway he turned and waved.

'Who was that?' I asked.

'Someone I nursed in 1983,' replied Ben.

Later we were walking through one of the small leafy parks in Tripoli when a man started shouting after us.

'Oh dear,' I said, 'not another of your patients!' Of course he was, and he insisted that we drink cup after cup of the coffee he was selling from an ornate three-foot-high brass coffee-pot. He made such a fuss of us that people began to gather round, which, incidentally, was good for his business.

'How is your leg?' asked Ben.

'Oh, I still get a lot of trouble from it,' he answered, squatting easily down on his haunches to wash the little china cups in a bucket.

After leaving Tripoli we travelled south to East Beirut,

where the expensive cars, well-dressed people and luxurious villas and apartment houses left no doubt as to which side of the city we were in. Late in the afternoon we crossed the Green Line back into West Beirut at the only open crossing point in the southern suburbs. We gave a lift to a beautiful dark Lebanese woman in a floral silk dress. As we queued in the exhaust fumes of the hundreds of other cars to cross the wasteland between the two checkpoints, she grumbled about the inconvenience to the daily lives of ordinary people who had to cross the Green Line every day for work.

It had been an idyllic four days. At last I had a sense of the history of this ancient land. I now knew what the Lebanon had been like and what it could be like if only the men who were its rulers could settle their differences and let the people live in peace.

Chapter 10

Lieve and Dirk left in late September. With their departure, the storm-clouds seemed to gather again. The news filtering in from the area around Sour was not good and the Palestinians feared that a new round of the Camp War would break out in the South. The tell-tale signs were there: increasing numbers of Palestinian men being taken away by Amal militiamen, the checkpoints around the refugee camp of Rashidiye becoming more strict, Palestinian families being intimidated into leaving their houses in the small camps on the coast just south of Rashidiye. When houses started being burned, many families fled north to the large Palestinian refugee camp of Ain al Hilweh in Saida, its population already swelled from approximately 50,000 to at least 60,000 by the exodus from the Beirut camps.

A friend of ours, a shop-owner in the camp, reappeared in Bourj al Barajneh. After the summer war he had closed up his shop in Bourj and taken his family to the more peaceful South but, as tension rose there, he came back to Beirut. We found him in the hospital. After a wedding, during which he had danced and drunk too much beer in the sunshine, he became dehydrated and was admitted to hospital with a severe sickle-cell crisis, a form of familial anaemia. He told us that a friendly Shiite from Sour had told him to go back north because there was trouble coming in the South.

The battle over the clinic had now been settled. The PRCS provided a new building about 50 metres from the old one. It was a two-storey building, slightly smaller than the old one, but with space for the primary health-care clinic downstairs, and two bedrooms and a living-room on the first floor. Ben painted the rooms blue and white, and Darwish, the fat, jolly plumber, fixed up the drainpipes and plumbed in the water-heater.

On 29 September, fighting began around Rashidiye, 80 kilometres south of Beirut. The people in Bourj al Barajneh were uneasy but did not think a fight would begin now with winter approaching. Dr Samer and I discussed the situation at Rashidiye. We knew they had no hospital there and wondered if we should go, and what sort of medical facilities we might improvise if we did. But, by the end of October, there were ominous signs in Beirut: the Amal militia were becoming more threatening every day. One morning I noticed that they had started to rebuild the sandhills around the camp. I was thankful that the thick fortification wall, being built to protect the lower floors of the hospital, was nearly finished.

Susie and Ben came back angry into the camp one afternoon. A couple of Amal militiamen had stopped them and tried to force them out of the ambulance just behind Akka Hospital. Ben, not wanting to repeat the experience of having an ambulance stolen from him, stubbornly refused to get out of the driving seat and Susie did likewise. As impatient drivers queued up behind the ambulance, hooting their horns, the Amal gunmen eventually relented and let them go.

A meeting of NORWAC and MAP staff was arranged for Wednesday 29 October in Hamra to discuss the problems of the team in the South. We debated whether or not to go. People in Bourj pleaded, 'Please don't leave the camp now,' but that day it was very quiet and although one man warned us, 'Today is not a good day,' the lookout at the edge of the camp waved to us cheerfully as we left at 2 p.m., saying that everything was quiet.

The team of four NORWAC and MAP members from the South were waiting for us in the flat. They had decided to evacuate from the South and felt bitter, angry and frustrated. Maureen, a Scottish physiotherapist, told us the story of the previous weeks. She had been working three mornings a week in a clinic at Rashidiye, and three mornings a week in a local Shiite village in co-operation with the Imam Musa Sadr Foundation. In the afternoons she made home visits to patients in the surrounding villages who were not able to come to her.

Although British, Maureen had managed to disguise the fact at checkpoints by describing herself as Scottish. 'Ah, yes,' one militiaman had said, 'Scotland, yes, that's near Australia, isn't it?' Movement had become more difficult as the checkpoints became more strict and eventually she was denied access to Rashidiye. The Palestinians were trying to build a makeshift hospital in the camp but, when they hired a bulldozer to dig foundations, Amal demanded it be brought back out and the building plans came to a halt.

Maureen managed to take in five boxes of medicines just before the fighting began, but she knew that the only health care centre in the camp was the small PRCS out-patient clinic staffed by a single GP.

The Amal militia fired occasionally into the camp of Bourj al Chemali, where the NORWAC team had lived. But then, the week before, they had twice burst into the flat and conducted a search. Although no one in the team was harmed, they were frightened by the aggression of the militiamen, who went up on to the roof and fired their guns into the air. Bourj al Chemali was an open camp with wide roads and not easily defended. The team of four felt threatened and unsafe and, no longer able to go to work, reluctantly decided to leave.

At a recent meeting of non-governmental organisations (mostly charities), Sol-Britt made plans for a survey of medical needs in the South. She thought that she herself could safely take a flat in Sour to do this work. From there she could monitor the situation to see when it would be safe for a team to go back to the South. I thought that this was an excellent idea. Sol-Britt knew her way around the Lebanon and was so calm and sensible that she would not be in any danger. She moved slowly, smiled a lot and never seemed a threat. What I did not know was that this was the last time I would see her in the Lebanon.

We left at 3.30 to be back in the camp by 4 p.m. Susie and Hannes took one ambulance and Ben and I took another. We picked up Dr Nader, one of the Palestinian GPs, from his sister's home in the city and on the way to the southern suburbs we saw Nadia, a nurse from the hospital, and gave her a lift too. We reached the airport road at 4 p.m. It was peaceful and traffic was flowing normally. At the checkpoint we chatted amicably with the Syrian soldiers who were there as observers. One of them was Kurdish and fond of Ben and always asked him about his 'wife'. I handed some antacid tablets to one of the others who had complained about his indigestion and we drove into the camp. We walked into the hospital via the emergency room entrance and I left Ben talking to the nurses while I went upstairs to collect something from my room.

Halfway up the stairs I heard the dreaded sound of people running and shouting, '*Ofta al tariek, ofta al tariek*,' which means 'Clear the way, clear the way.' I ran downstairs again, just as four stretcher-bearers were bringing in a man with blood all over his face. The hospital had one of its frequent power-cuts so there was no light in the emergency room. They put him down on the floor so that I could look at him in the half-light of the entrance.

I knelt on the floor. His mouth was full of blood and he had no pulse. I scooped out the clotted blood from his mouth and throat and started mouth-to-mouth resuscitation. Then I shouted for the intubation set to pass a breathing tube down his throat. Beside me, someone was already doing heart massage. In the dim light I could not tell at first that it was Ben. Someone else was trying to set up a drip. I could feel a warm trickle of blood soaking through my trousers to my knee. People were crowding round, blocking out even more light, so I shouted that we must take him into the operating-room area, where I knew there was a battery-operated tungsten light. I also wanted a chance to assess the man away from the hysteria in the entrance hall.

Two men lifted him on the stretcher and carried him into the operating room. There I tried again to clear out his mouth and looked down his throat with the laryngoscope to see if I could pass a breathing tube. I saw at once that all the structures in the throat were totally destroyed. There was a small bullet-entry wound on the left side of his neck and a larger exit wound on the right. It was a typical high-velocity M-16 wound. All our attempts to revive him were useless. He was completely dead.

By this time we could hear fierce fighting going on at the top of the camp. Within minutes it spread all around the perimeter. Ben quickly decided to go down to the clinic to join Hannes and Susie and to set up a first-aid post. When there was a lull in the fighting he dashed off.

I stayed in the hospital and, with Salah the head nurse and Dr Samer, prepared the emergency room to receive more wounded. The nurses' desk was moved out of the way against the wall, the four couches were pulled out from the walls to allow access to both sides and both ends of the patients, drips for resuscitation were made ready and we checked and replenished the equipment on the shelves. When I went out into the corridor, families were moving into the hospital with small collections of belongings. The two old men who had stayed during the summer war appeared again with their bedrolls and settled down in their old places in the stair-well. 'Oh no,' I thought, 'it's all beginning again.'

Dr Rede was not in the camp. He had gone out to a meeting of the PRCS. There were five doctors in Bourj al Barajneh: myself, the only surgeon; Dr Samer, who by now was experienced from his work in the summer war and whom I knew I could rely on and who would work hard; Dr Nader, a GP; Dr Aissam, an obstetrician, who had returned to his family in the camp 10 days before, after completing his training in the USSR; and Dr Dergham, a GP and junior physician. Dr Dergham hated surgery and disliked dealing with blood and wounds. People told me contemptuously that previously he had kept away from this work as much as possible. But that night he came to the emergency room and asked us to tell him what to do. He did everything he was instructed, starting with the minor wounds. Despite the scorn of one or two of the nurses, he worked with us. I admired him for it and encouraged him. The other hospital workers, off duty in the camp, came running as soon as they heard the shooting.

After supper at around 7 p.m., I was going downstairs to the emergency room when I saw Hassan walking out of the hospital with his Kalashnikov over his shoulder.

'It is a very heavy attack,' he told me. 'I must go and help.'

'Please take care,' I said.

A few minutes later, his mother came in enquiring anxiously about him. 'Have you seen him?' she asked me.

'I saw him here a few minutes ago,' I said. I didn't have the heart to tell her he had gone to fight, although I think she suspected.

An hour later, Hassan was brought back in, shot through the right upper arm. I felt his pulse which was present but weak. We splinted his arm, gave him an injection for pain and arranged for an X-ray. He was distraught and crying with pain, but had his gun still firmly gripped in his left hand and was refusing to relinquish it.

'Hassan,' I implored, 'you're going to the X-ray room. You do not need your gun. Put it down.'

'No, no, no!' he shouted, struggling with someone who was trying to take it away from him.

I knew he would part with his gun when he calmed down,

so we sent him off to X-ray still clutching it. He gave it up after the X-ray.

The bone was not broken and the nerves were working, but the pulse had become impalpable. If the blood-vessel was damaged, Hassan could lose his arm, so I told him we must operate to explore the artery. I thought he had been rather irresponsible to go to the front line when his duty was here in the operating-theatre, but I was dearly fond of him and was desperately concerned to save his arm. Dr Samer, eager to work in the operating-theatre, wanted to assist but, as the most experienced of the others, agreed to stay in the emergency room. I took Dr Nader.

The artery was only in spasm, tightly contracted because of the force of the bullet, and after the application of some warm saline and local anaesthetic the pulse rapidly picked up. Hassan was lucky. Pure spasm is quite rare. Most arteries suspected of being damaged *are* damaged.

When we came out of the operating-theatre, Hassan's mother was waiting anxiously outside. I told her not to worry and that the wound was relatively minor. She hugged me before I could take off my blood-stained operating clothes.

The news of Hassan's injury had spread throughout the hospital. As I walked upstairs, one of the older women who worked in the hospital, the mother of a teenage fighter, took me aside. She said, with tears in her eyes, 'I don't want my son to fight. I want him to go to university, not be killed in the front line. But although I fear for his life, I am proud and glad when he takes up his gun, because I know he goes to defend us Palestinians as a people.'

Another of the women who worked in the kitchen, her face thin and lined with worry beneath her grey scarf, joined in. 'I have three sons fighting,' she said. 'What should I do? Should I tell them to sit at home when we are attacked?'

I knew one of her sons; he had been wounded in the face and jaw in the summer war but was back now at the front

In the doctors' room after operating all day.

Bourj al Barajneh camp. On the skyline is the devastated Haifa Hospital.

Ziad the beggar (right) and his family in their house.

Haifa Hospital after the siege.

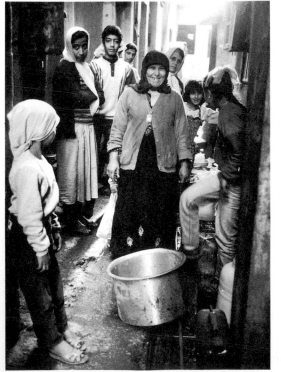

Queuing for water. A week later the woman in the centre was shot in the leg.

With Dirk (left) and Lieve in the emergency room.

Hussein dancing at his sister's wedding.

In the operating-theatre.

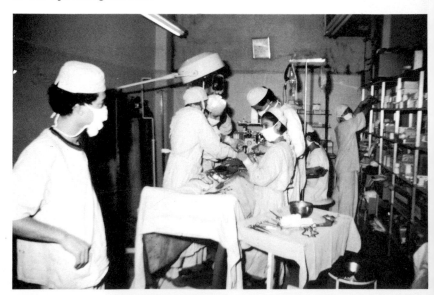

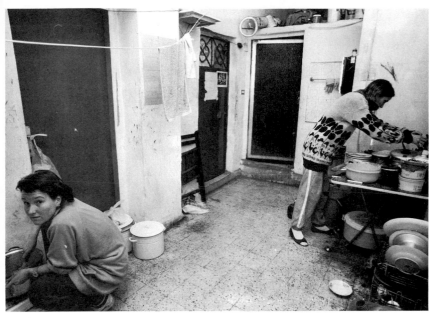

With Susie in the kitchen at the clinic.

Women waiting for permission to leave the camp at the end of the siege.

A woman is shot coming back into the camp.

In the emergency room, we fight to save her life. *Left to right:* Dr Mounir, Dr Rede, Salah (with moustache).

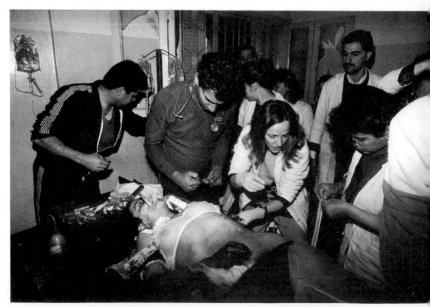

Women carry the wounded woman out of the camp to hospital.

Fighters on the perimeter of the camp.

With Susie at Jounieh waiting to leave for Cyprus

With Susie and Ben arriving at Heathrow airport.

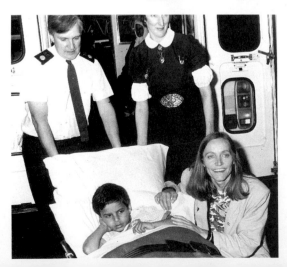

Bilal arrives, on his way to Stoke Mandeville hospital.

line. He was a very handsome, dignified young man, mature for his 22 years, who came to see me from time to time to ask me to revise the unsightly scar across half his face. It could undoubtedly be improved, but it was still too fresh and he agreed to wait patiently.

After checking to see that Hassan was recovering from his anaesthetic, I went up to bed. I put my mattress on the floor and tried to position the wardrobe between me and the window, but at an angle, so that it would offer some protection but wouldn't fall on top of me.

The fighting continued all night and into the next day, but it was mostly shooting with only a few bombs. In the morning, the other doctors and I did a ward round. Patients with minor wounds from the day before were sent home. Hassan's arm was fine. I urged him to stay in hospital for another day, but he protested, saying he was fine and wanted to go home. Later in the day he couldn't bear to wait any longer and went home of his own accord. He lived very close by and I knew he would be all right.

There were still patients in the hospital from before the fighting, among them a young, beautiful, dark-haired, half-Palestinian, half-Syrian girl with two broken legs, now being skin-grafted, and a thirteen-year-old girl, Fatme, from Sour in the south. She was a Lebanese Shiite girl from a poor family, who was having a series of operations on her legs to correct deformities due to polio. She had come to Haifa for free treatment, unable to pay for private treatment, and her mother was staying with her in the hospital. There was also an ancient, white-haired, bird-like lady who had a plaster on her arm after an operation on her elbow. They too had to be taken care of.

Also in the hospital, whenever there was fighting, were the paraplegics, brought over from their house. They were put up where there was room.

About 30 families were now sheltering in the entrance hall and in the shelter in the other wing of the hospital, and showed no signs of going home. My experience from the summer war was that their sixth sense would tell them when it was safe, so they were like a sort of barometer for me.

Dr Samer and I made contingency plans in case the fighting went on for weeks as it had done in the summer. We knew that the hospital was well stocked. A three-month store of medicines and equipment had been stockpiled. I asked for a full inventory from the pharmacists and we issued instructions to the nurses not to be extravagant with gauze and to keep all potentially reusable materials such as crepe bandages and chest tube bottles.

That morning I saw a group of Syrian soldiers from the buffer force hanging around the emergency room and the hospital entrance, easily recognisable because of the pink patches in their camouflage uniforms. They, and several Lebanese soldiers, had run into the camp for safety when the shooting broke out yesterday. We treated a few more minor wounds. Then, in the afternoon, an old man, who was said to be 100 years old, came in with a few shrapnel wounds, one in the chest which required a chest tube drain. He had a rare blood group but his granddaughter, one of the nurses, was the same group and was able to donate him a pint of blood.

All day, men were streaming past the hospital to take up their posts on the perimeter. Among them I saw young boy-soldiers with guns; some of them could not have been older than 12 or 13. One of the older men explained to me: 'This is the reality of their lives. They grow up in an atmosphere of violence and fighting, and they want to be like their fathers and brothers. They do not fight now but they go to the front line to learn the discipline and not to be afraid because they will be the next generation who will have to defend us. It is safer for them later if they learn now.'

During one heavy round of fighting a young, fair, curly-haired boy, who looked about 15 years old and was even smaller than me, ran in to the hospital entrance in his new military outfit and sat down on the bench, holding his gun. He was sweating profusely and breathing deeply. I felt sorry for him. He was obviously terrified and he sat and stared out of the doorway into the dust without speaking. After five or so minutes he got up, took a deep breath, gritted his teeth and ran back out. I often saw him again, but never frightened like that first time.

At about 5 p.m., there was a big commotion in the emergency room. A young man was brought in shot through the head. He was still breathing. We put up a drip and gave him some medicines. Some of the senior military men arrived and while he was being X-rayed they managed to negotiate via their walkie-talkie radios to have him transferred to a neurosurgery unit. After he was taken away, I noticed that many people were gloomy. Apparently, he was one of the chief officers in the pro-Syrian Palestinian groups who had ventured to the edge of the camp to try to negotiate a ceasefire. It did not bode well that he was shot. We learned later that he died in the emergency room of the American University Hospital.

Ben came up to visit in the evening. He had heard the fighting around Bourj mentioned on the Lebanese news in English. Rashidiye in the South was still under siege and there were even some clashes reported from Saida. Amal were firing into the refugee camp of Ain al Hilweh from a Christian town called Magdoushe, situated on a hill overlooking Saida and the camp.

Susie and Ben had set up a first-aid station on the ground floor of the clinic and had already treated several patients. Although the stretcher-bearers were used to transporting the wounded, and some of them were trained in first aid, a few still had a tendency to panic and race straight to the hospital. Ben had stopped a group going past with a man whose broken arm was dangling over the side of the stretcher. That could do untold harm. Fortunately Ben saw them and made them wait while he splinted the arm and stopped the bleeding, so the man had arrived at the hospital in a good and stable condition.

On advice from the Palestinians, Susie had also moved their sleeping-bags, and all the belongings they required for their immediate needs, downstairs, so they were sleeping in relative safety.

The next morning, 31 October, I got up at 8 a.m. and found Dr Samer in the emergency room. He had the nurses organised into moving everything around. 'Perhaps he should have discussed this first,' was my immediate thought but I looked around at what he was doing and it was excellent. He and Salah had opened up a small adjoining room, thus enlarging the emergency area which could now accommodate six couches when the nurses' desk was pushed out of the way and some cupboards shifted. I suggested that we put the couches against the outer wall so that the doorways were all in a line, providing wide, clear access for the stretchers to all the rooms. To do this, two more sturdy cupboards and an X-ray viewing box had to be moved.

It was sometimes difficult to motivate the nurses to do such work, but that morning we were all infected by Dr Samer's enthusiasm and they even went on to clean everything when we were finished. It was a great improvement. Dr Samer and I looked at each other and laughed. There had been a recent plan from the chiefs to make the emergency area smaller and install a very big nurses' desk. We decided that we would never let them go back to that plan.

The camp was still completely closed. There was a lot of shooting around the perimeter but little bombing. The 100-year-old man died. At that age a chest wound is almost invariably fatal.

There were a few injuries in the fighting, but none too serious. We were concerned about a man in his sixties who was admitted with severe congestive heart failure. His face and his extremities were swollen and blue and he made a bubbling sound when he breathed. Confused and barely conscious, he upset the nurses by peeing against the wall in the corner of his room. I suspected that he had run out of his routine medicines, but he was incoherent and unable to tell us anything. We did what investigations were possible, but the new equipment ordered for Haifa had not yet arrived so still the only blood test available was a basic blood count. With a little oxygen and some drugs he improved slightly by evening, but he remained gravely ill.

The following morning another old man was brought in dead. I recognised him by his few remaining teeth and his checked scarf around his head. It was Abu Arab, a chronic asthmatic. I thought of Dirk, who had treated many of his asthmatic attacks and eventually stabilised him on some new long-acting medicines; I knew he would be very sad to hear of his death. He must have had a severe attack and had not sought treatment quickly enough. He and the old man from the day before were as much casualties of this war as the wounded fighters. The stress of the fighting made them ill and the fear of going out of doors prevented them from seeking treatment until it was too late.

Later that morning a ceasefire was declared. The man with heart failure could go out and Dr Rede and Dr Ataya were able to come in.

Dr Rede was relieved that we had not been overwhelmed with wounded. 'I was worried at first that no surgeon was in the camp,' he said. 'I tried to get in on Wednesday at quarter past four [which was only 15 minutes after we had entered uneventfully] but I found all the roads closed by Amal militiamen. After two hours worrying, I phoned Sol-Britt at the flat and, when she said you weren't there, I guessed you must be in the camp.'

The evening was fairly calm, so I was able to take a break from the hospital for an hour and run down to the clinic where Ben cooked some hot and filling custard for us. We told each other about our experiences during the day and shared the rumours we had each picked up on the grapevine.

Hannes did not like going backwards and forwards between the hospital and the clinic where he was sleeping. It was too dangerous. So he moved in to the hospital and slept in a small consultation room next to the physiotherapy room.

The following day was also fairly calm with only one serious injury. I let Dr Samer repair the torn artery in the man's arm while I assisted. He did it beautifully and was delighted with himself, having been itching to do some more operating. I knew it was important to teach him, and the others, as much as I possibly could, because there might come a time when he would have to deal with these wounds on his own. Dr Rede organised the three GPs, Dr Dergham, Dr Nader and Dr Samer, to do daily out-patient clinics on a 1 in 3 rota and once again we formed four emergency teams.

That evening, Ben came complaining of backache. Some shells had exploded near the clinic and he had been busy with friends putting up sandbags at the windows to stop breaking glass or shrapnel flying in. (We had been doing the same thing at the hospital.) He had put his back out while lugging about the heavy sandbags.

These precautions seemed rather premature when, two days later on 4 November, another ceasefire was declared and a peace agreement announced on the radio. The Syrian soldiers must have left the camp that day because I never saw them again. The morning was quiet and, at lunchtime, Ben was asked to take two patients out of the camp in the NORWAC ambulance. But, like so many ceasefires, this one was short-lived and, half an hour after Ben left, a sudden heavy bombardment began.

I ran down to the emergency room where the wounded were already arriving. The first 15 came almost together. Even our enlarged emergency room was completely inadequate.

Most of the wounded were children. A bomb had landed in a yard where they were playing and they all had shrapnel injuries. There were not enough stretchers and adults were running in with injured children in their arms. There were wounded people everywhere, on the floor, in the entrance hall, in the corridor. On each couch lay two or three bleeding children, and the room was full of hysterical parents and relatives. We later called this 'The Day of the Children'.

For a moment in the confusion I felt only anger that this bloodshed and horrible cruelty was inflicted on these children who had no way to escape it, but I was soon too busy sorting them out to think about anything else.

Three children and one adult were dead and one adult was dying. Dr Rede took all the children with minor wounds upstairs, while the rest of us dealt with the more serious injuries and put them in order of priority for X-ray, blood transfusion and operation.

We operated all the rest of the day, through the night and well into the following morning. While we were operating, more wounded arrived. In total that day, 5 people died and 25 were wounded.

The following day, 5 November, was not much better. I managed to speak to Ben at lunchtime on the walkie-talkie in the administrator's room. He was at the PRCS headquarters in Mar Elias and was very frustrated at being stuck outside. I dreaded the thought that the fighting might drag on like the summer war and I would not see Ben for weeks. I had not seen Susie and hoped she was coping on her own in the first-aid clinic.

In the late afternoon, as I was operating on a man with an abdominal wound, one of the nurses from the emergency room brought in a message that Susie was wounded. As soon as we finished operating, I ran out and found Susie lying on a couch in the emergency room, smiling and protesting that it was only a scratch. I looked at her X-ray and at the wound in her arm. Thank God it was only minor. There was a small piece of shrapnel deep in the forearm, lying between the radius and ulna, but it would do no harm and I decided it should be left alone.

'*Hamdullilah es salami*,' I told her, which means 'Thank God for your good health'. '*Allahsalmik*,' she replied, which means 'Thank God for yours, too'.

The wound was cleaned and dressed and her arm put in a sling. Ben was still outside the camp, so Susie had been on her own in the first-aid clinic. She was insisting on going straight back to work. I had to get Dr Rede to order her to rest for one night in the hospital. Our friend Ahmed had been wounded with Susie, but his injuries were also minor. They were making tea in the front room of the clinic when a shell exploded in the square in front of the building and small pieces of shrapnel flew in through the already broken window. After that, they moved all the tea-making equipment into the back room.

Later that night, an entire family was brought in. Their house had been hit by a shell. The father came up to me. It was Darwish, our local plumber. He and his son had minor wounds, his daughter had a chest wound and his wife, the most serious, had a severe head wound exposing the brain and pieces of shrapnel deep inside. Contact was made with the Amal militia by walkie-talkie, but the answer was a firm 'no'; she would not be allowed to a hospital outside.

We had two alternatives. Either we could operate on her or we could leave her to die. None of us had ever done any neurosurgery before, although I knew the theory and Dr Rede had assisted in neurosurgical operations some years before. We discussed it with Darwish and decided to operate.

I operated and Dr Rede assisted. I was very apprehensive and we had only very crude instruments for such delicate surgery. The most useful help came from Nooha, the 26-year-old nurse in charge of the operating-theatre. An extremely well-trained and experienced theatre nurse, who had worked in London and Paris, she had seen much neuro-surgery, and was able to advise us. 'You should make that hole a bit bigger,' she said as I gingerly cut my way into the womans head. 'It will make it easier.' Very delicately we picked out pieces of shrapnel and fragments of shattered bone with forceps. Then we removed the dead brain tissue with low-powered suction apparatus. One by one we stopped the small vessels bleeding. There was still a slight trickle. 'You can stop that bleeding with a pack of Gelfoam and hydrogen peroxide solution,' said Nooha.

The operation took five hours, but we were concentrating so hard that it seemed like only an hour had passed when we finished at 4.30 in the morning. Time always passed incredibly quickly when I was operating. It demanded total concentration, but that always seemed possible even when I was exhausted. Only when the patient was waking up and the final check had been made did I become aware of the back-ache, stiffness and tiredness. But if I had operated on patients one after the other it was difficult to remember who had what and whether the operation was during the day or at night. I never got to the point where I couldn't go on, but I think I was close.

Darwish's wife eventually recovered. Any credit for her unexpected survival belongs to Nooha.

I slept late and was woken up by a knock on my door. It was Ben. Miraculously, he and a Palestinian driver of a PRCS car were allowed back into the camp by the Syrian and Lebanese soldiers at the airport road. They had told them, 'Drive fast because there are snipers.' Ben and his friend had sped across the 100 metres of open ground with their heads down, expecting a bullet at any moment.

While outside, he had delivered a patient from Mar Elias to Akka Hospital, which was still just functioning. Akka was only about a kilometre from Bourj al Barajneh and from the top of the building, five floors up, he had angrily watched tanks bombarding the camp from behind the sandhills. After a cup of tea he went down to the clinic to see how Susie was and how she was managing with her wounded arm.

During the following week, the fighting increased in intensity. Electricity was cut off completely from the whole camp and we had to rely on the two diesel-powered generators in the hospital. One was big and could provide enough power for the whole hospital and more, but the other was smaller and could only run for a few hours at a time. People used kerosene lamps, candles and torches to light their homes, and cooked with bottled gas. There was a lull at the beginning of the week and we were able to send out Darwish's wife, two days after her operation, but after that the seige tightened and the camp remained completely closed.

Every so often the hospital was hit. In one attack the water tank was damaged. Water trickled down the walls and dripped from the ceilings in all the rooms. It ran down the stairs into the corridors, collecting, inches deep in some places. It was impossible to keep your feet dry. The women cleaners spent long hours every day sweeping the water out of the rooms and corridors, while the men built a small brick and concrete dam at the top of the stairs on the first floor, just outside my room. They diverted the worst of the flood along a channel and out over a balcony. The problem was compounded by the rains, which had now begun.

On 11 November, I wrote in my diary: 'Sporadic bombing and shooting all day again. Every time I think I can go down to the clinic for an hour's break, all hell breaks loose and more wounded come so I think I cannot go until all is really calm. It has been very cold and wet for about four or five days now. My roof and windows are leaking and the floor is awash. Not only do my clothes not dry, but the dry ones are getting wet. I dream of sitting in front of a coal fire and long for stew and dumplings. I hope there will be a solution for this bloody war because I have had enough. Also, I worry about Ben down in the clinic. Many bombs have landed on the adjacent buildings. When the three dead came today, I had a cold feeling in my stomach and a temptation to look under the blankets to make sure one was not Ben.'

This strange, uncanny feeling helped me to understand why it was impossible to keep out of the emergency room people who were desperate to see their wounded relatives.

The BBC World Service made brief mention of outbreaks of fighting, but also gave us some good news. The old Frenchman, Camil Sonntag, had been released with another hostage and was in Damascus. I passed the message on to Ali who was very pleased for him.

Dr Rede, Dr Mounir and I were operating almost every day and I did not always have time to eat very well. Because of the lack of electricity, Ben and Susie were no longer able to sterilise in the clinic and had to bring gauze and instruments to the hospital daily to put in the dry heaters when the generator was on. Ben came most evenings and he kept my spirits up. He had to run up the hill from the clinic because of the dangers of bombing but he still often brought hot custard or pancakes with him which Hannes and Muntaha also enjoyed. Muntaha was a nurse whose family home was outside the camp. She came in during the first days of the war because she knew she would be needed and after that she just lived in the hospital. I could never sleep for 20 minutes after Ben left in the evenings until I could be sure he was safely in the clinic. If he had been hurt, he would have been back in the hospital on a stretcher.

Each day the bombardment of the camp seemed to grow heavier and more prolonged. And it appeared that the hospital was now a deliberate target. On 15 November, after a particularly bad day, during which shrapnel had smashed through the windows of my room, I moved down to the operating-theatre ante-room in the basement with the theatre staff, as did Dr Rede. There were now 10 of us living in that small area. We did not sleep in the actual operating room, but three of us slept on fold-up camp-beds by the sinks in the scrubbing-up room, which measured 3 metres by 2 metres. The other seven were sleeping on camp-beds and mattresses in the outer sterilising and store-room, about 5 metres by 3 metres. The beds and mattresses were folded up during the day and taken out at night. It was much warmer down there and there was an atmosphere of friendly coexistence but the lack of privacy was sometimes a strain.

My only change of clothing when I went to bed was to take off my wet socks and hang them on a drip stand, hoping they would dry a bit by the morning. The leaders of the political factions (like the PLO) had brought clothes for those people with no family homes in the camp. Each person was issued with a pair of pyjamas, which most of us now were wearing under our clothes, a track suit, towels, socks and new plastic baseball-style boots. These were a godsend. Wearing the boots my feet were wet only half the time. Nooha sometimes dried the boots for me on top of the dry heater when it was sterilising instruments.

Susie and Ben were fine. Susie was tough and never complained about her arm. Although she still had restricted movement in two of the fingers she was back to full work. She and Ben had now withdrawn to one room for living, working and sleeping and she told me even there at times they had to sit on the floor against the inner wall during the intense bombing. They had no electricity but a bright kerosene pressure lamp. They were getting food from the kitchen that made food for the fighters.

It was very rewarding to see the children recovering. They get better so much quicker than adults and by the end of the week most of them, even those with big operations, were running around and ready to go home.

But no sooner were the first batch of children better than some more were wounded. An 18-month-old girl was blinded. A jagged piece of shrapnel, the size of a peanut, passed through one eye, crossed behind her nose and damaged the other eye, coming to rest just beneath it. Her six-year-old sister died in the same blast. Two eleven-year-old boys, cousins, were also wounded. One was hit in the head and his brain exposed, the other in the chest and abdomen. By now there was no chance of sending anyone out. I operated on the two boys one after the other. The heavy bombardment continued during the operations until at last they started shelling the Amal positions from the mountains. Then, like before, it stopped immediately.

The little boy with the chest and abdominal wounds was dismayed by his eight tubes when he woke up the next day. He counted them with a solemn face as I removed them one by one over the next week. He tried to behave in a grown-up way, with a frown on his forehead but never crying, as I did his dressings, but by the end of the week he could not resist smiling and giggling as he helped me take out his own stitches. The other little boy got better more slowly. In the first few days, if he was disturbed, he let out an abnormal cry, like a cat. Eventually he was able to speak to us, but refused to open his eyes. His brain injury had not upset the English he had learned at school and he would say 'Good morning' to me and 'I'm fine, thank you.' He was very wobbly when he first began to walk after 10 days and he retained a tremor of his right hand whenever he tried to use it but otherwise he eventually made a remarkable recovery.

The hospital now had about 45 in-patients and we had to open the rooms in the shelter again and another large area next to them, though it was not well ventilated as it had no windows. Four of the paraplegics were moved down to one of the hospital rooms as well. One night, Muntaha, the nurse, had nowhere to sleep and no one realised until Dr Samer found her walking the corridor at 3 a.m. and demanded that Salah find her a bed somewhere.

Mashour, a bearded nurse with strict Muslim beliefs, worked in the emergency room. He had not shaken my hand when I first met him, and generally he did not touch women nor did his wife touch men. But he was a terrible hypochondriac and his aches and pains did not stop during the fighting. He and I had a very good working relationship and developed a good friendship. Occasionally I examined him, his rib which hurt here or his shoulder which hurt when he did that, or his abdomen when he had a bad stomach-ache. Then the no-touch rule did not apply. He often asked me to see and treat his wife and two small children who were living with him in a store cupboard in the hospital and on whose behalf he was also rather hypochondriacal.

By the end of November, people in the camp were talking about a long siege. Bourj al Barajneh had been under attack for a month and Rashidiye for two months. News filtering through from Rashidiye was bad. People there were becoming desperate and it was reported on the Monte Carlo news in Arabic that they were eating grass and weeds. The Amal militia would not lift the siege of Rashidiye until the situation in Beirut had been settled. But in Beirut there was no sign of peace and on 29 November the fighting spread to Chatila.

When one of the Palestinian political leaders came to the operating room one night to see how we were and what we needed, Nooha asked him how long the siege would go on. He replied, 'Ninety days, I think.'

'Ninety days!' we said in mock horror. We thought he was joking.

'That's nothing,' said Ben. 'When Alexander the Great laid siege to Tyre, it was seven months before the city fell.' We all laughed again.

In Bourj al Barajneh camp, people were being killed at the rate of one a day. After living here a year I knew many of them. Dr Rede had been born and brought up in Bourj camp and was sometimes almost immobilised with grief when a relative or close friend died. But the Amal militia were losing even more men.

The Palestinians were defending the camp from positions in the houses overlooking the outlying streets at the bottom of the hill or the open ground at the top of the hill. Occasionally, the Amal militia would make an Iranian style 'human wave' attack. One Palestinian fighter told me it was a terrible sight. Twenty men would charge across the street and just be mown down. Maybe 10 or 15 would be killed at a time, and the wounded had to lie and wait for ambulances. We could sometimes hear their sirens, and occasionally the radio announced that hospitals were in urgent need of blood.

Despite the primitive nature of Haifa Hospital, in some ways we were better off than Amal. The wounded did not have to wait for ambulances. Their family and friends supplied fresh warm blood which was of the best quality and, if more was needed, the mosque loudspeaker would announce it and others would come to donate their blood.

Let me give two examples. One was a young woman brought in on 18 November. A man brought her in wrapped in a blanket over his shoulder, thinking she was dead. I looked at her; her skin was the translucent white of someone who had bled to death and she had a two-centimetre shrapnel wound in the groin. Then she gasped, once, and I realised that she was not quite dead. I shouted for the intubation set and some help. She had no pulse but with my stethoscope I could hear a faint heartbeat. Her veins were completely empty of blood and after passing a breathing tube down her throat I began cutting into the skin to find a vein to put up a drip. Dr Samer came to help and within a couple of minutes we had three drips up. While we were working frantically, I noticed a man standing quietly behind me. It was Abu Taissir, the kindly grey-haired man who used to come and play cards with us and often came to the hospital to see what he could do to help.

'What does she need?' he asked.

'She needs blood quickly,' I replied.

After five minutes, the transfusion was ready and we filled her up with blood. The wound in the groin immediately began to bleed again. We pressed a gauze pad into it, and keeping the pressure on, rushed her into the operating-theatre. Someone had to stand pressing the wound while we washed briefly and put on gloves and gowns. Enlarging the wound, I was able to clamp the ends of the completely cut artery and vein to the leg and thus control the bleeding. As we worked, one of the nurses told me she was Abu Taissir's daughter. I was stunned. He had been so calm. Although she did not regain consciousness for two days, she eventually recovered completely.

The other example was a young man who came on 28 November with multiple shrapnel wounds from a bomb that had exploded behind him. There was shrapnel in his chest and his abdomen. The operation revealed that every organ, including the vena cava, the main vein of the body, was holed by shrapnel, and from head to feet his flesh was full of at least 500 small pieces of shrapnel. He bled profusely and we gave him 12 pints of blood (the normal body has only 8). It took hours to stitch up all the holes inside and take out a kidney, but he also survived.

Only because we were able to give large quantities of

fresh warm blood – and so soon after injury – did these two survive. I am sure that outside, waiting for ambulances, they would have died.

What a futile, calamitous war this was for the local Shiite population outside the camp. Their leader, Nabih Berri, may have had political and power gains to make, especially by having the support of the Syrians. But, for the local inhabitants, it was a disaster. Their young men were dying. Their trade with the Palestinians from local shops and businesses was gone. Their buildings and houses which they had to abandon were damaged and destroyed. The Palestine Red Crescent Society free health service, now associated with their enemy, they were no longer able to use.

By now the hospital building was taking heavy punishment. All the remaining windows were smashed and one bomb, which landed just outside the front entrance, took off the foot of a girl playing in the doorway and peppered one of the NORWAC ambulances parked outside. After a prolonged bombardment by tanks one afternoon, the whole of the top floor of the hospital, the fourth floor, finally collapsed completely. It was reported on the radio that Amal had announced they had taken control of Haifa Hospital!

Abu Taissir's daughter, recovering from her shrapnel wounds, escaped death again when a tank shell ploughed through the wall of the ground-floor ward, showering her and her sister with rubble but not harming them.

I was sometimes able to talk to the new NORWAC co-ordinator, Øyvind, on the walkie-talkie, when he contacted us from Mar Elias, to tell him that we were all right. It was possible for outsiders to listen in and interfere with the conversations, so I was not supposed to use my name. My code-name, I discovered to my amusement, was The Blonde.

Despite repeated efforts we were not allowed to send out

the blind toddler. Dr Mounir looked after her carefully, cleaning the eyes every day and applying ointment to prevent infection. Then, after two weeks, she opened her eyes slightly and it became apparent that she could see from one eye. If you moved an object in front of her, she would follow it with her head. Hannes cried. He told me afterwards that he had been praying for the child.

In quiet moments I sometimes sat with Nooha. Conscientious and aware of her responsibility of being in charge, she rarely left the operating-theatre. She always wore her scarf, even in the operating room. One afternoon her mother came to bring her some clean clothes and when she left I asked Nooha about the rest of her family. A sister and brother lived with their mother in the camp, but her father and her other sister had been killed four years before in the Israeli invasion of 1982. 'They were both killed in one afternoon,' she said. 'My sister died when the building she was in collapsed during an Israeli air raid. It was hit by a vacuum bomb. When she did not return home my father went to look for her. He found her dead. On the way home he was killed by a car bomb probably planted by the Christian Phalangists.

'After that I decided that I would never marry and have children. I saw what it had done to my mother. In this country, too many children die, too many husbands . . .'

I didn't know what to say to her. Perhaps she was right.

'I thought I would go on working as a nurse,' she continued, 'but even that was difficult. The Israelis smashed everything to pieces. When Gaza was rebuilt, everything was fine for a while, but then Amal came.'

I knew what had happened at Gaza Hospital. Amal had entered the hospital, chased out the patients and staff, looted the equipment and set fire to the building. 'And now the same fate is about to befall Haifa Hospital,' I thought, but I didn't say it aloud and tried to put the idea out of my mind.

Chapter 11

At the end of November, after two months of siege, conditions in Rashidiye camp were grim. Rumours reached us that they were now desperately short of food; the one solitary doctor was exhausted and patients were dying of gangrene. The unrelenting military assault on Bourj al Barajneh was grindingly oppressive and Chatila was being pounded to rubble. Palestinian forces had gone out from Ain el Hilweh, the big camp in Saida, and taken the town of Magdoushe from Amal to try to gain bargaining power with which to force Amal into lifting the siege of Rashidiye. But the fighting only got worse. Amal tried to retake Magdoushe, a Catholic Christian town on the hill overlooking Saida. Most of the inhabitants were leaving to get away from the fighting. It was reported that Amal militiamen accused the Christians living there of siding with the Palestinians and had killed four of them. Two were shot and two hacked to death with an axe.

In the South, around Sour, the Palestinians were being driven out and sought safety in Saida. The Lebanese news in English reported that 200 houses in the small Palestinian camp of Jim Jim were burned down. Nabih Berri was in Damascus and the news spoke of peace talks, but to me they sounded more like war talks. The bombing continued.

In West Beirut city which now to me, unable to leave the camp, seemed far away, there was some unrest. On 2 December there was a general strike, which lasted for a day, to protest against the worsening economic situation. For the first 10 years of civil war, the Lebanese pound had remained remarkably stable, but in the last year it had sunk from 20 to the dollar to 70 to the dollar. So inflation had taken off.

We listened obsessively to all these news broadcasts in the hope of hearing of a breakthrough to end the Camp War and we all endlessly discussed 'the situation'. It was the first thing we talked about over breakfast and the last thing we talked about at night. Everybody had their own ideas and forecasts. Optimists would announce that peace was at hand and the war would be over within a week. Others, like Dr Dergham, were very pessimistic. He blamed the political and military leaders and reckoned that the war would only be solved when the people got rid of them all.

The accuracy of news broadcasts could not always be relied upon. On 3 December the Lebanese news reported that Red Cross cars had entered Rashidiye, but news from the walkie-talkie grapevine came to Dr Rede and he said it was not true. Dr Rede was scrupulously honest and realistic and I relied very much upon what he told us. He could see no immediate end to the conflict.

Even the camp of Ain el Hilweh in Saida was not free from bloodshed. On 4 December Israeli helicopter gunships bombed the camp and Mieh-Mieh camp nearby. These air raids were not unusual, occurring about once a fortnight, but at this time it seemed a vicious and pitiless act of violence as we knew that these so called 'military targets' were packed with Palestinian families seeking sanctuary. On 11 December, Israeli jets bombed a Palestinian camp in Tripoli, in northern Lebanon, killing 15 people.

Meanwhile, in Bourj al Barajneh, little in our everyday lives changed. At the hospital we were still busy with wounded and operating every day. Those changes that did occur were usually for the worse. To conserve fuel the generators were running four hours on, four hours off, just long enough to keep the blood and medicine fridges cold. Candles and fuel for lamps were in short supply so, when the generators were off, the hospital was a dim and dark place even in the daytime, with the sandbags blocking up the windows.

The cold winds and rains of winter were well set in. The hospital leaked very badly and water continued to dribble down the walls, collecting in pools on the floors. Most rooms were growing mould and even in the operating-theatre a green and black slime was creeping down one wall, re-appearing within hours of being wiped off. The sandbags kept out the shrapnel but not the wind, and Hannes remarked that his room was a wind tunnel and sometimes his precious candle blew out.

Ben was not very well. He had amoebic dysentery and was taking medicines. Because electricity was cut off from the camp, water was no longer pumped into the houses. It had to be collected from taps in the streets, which carried water from outside to about 10 points around the camp. Some of this water was probably contaminated. There were a few wells in the camp but again the water could not be pumped up without electricity.

The GPs' clinics were becoming more crowded with people suffering from diarrhoea. Other common complaints were colds, flu, coughs and bronchitis, and we admitted a few cases of pneumonia. Fresh fruit and vegetables had long ago run out. All that was left was a few potatoes and onions, and with the consequent lack of vitamin C in the diet it was difficult to shake off these common ailments.

Despite the increasing hardships, we remained fairly cheerful. There was an unshakeable community spirit and people rallied round to help each other. Many, especially our friends, were kind and generous to us. When Hassan's mother and Dr Samer's saw me in blood-stained outfits, both offered to wash my clothes. Unfortunately, most of my clothes were now eaten away by mould, but Fatme, Souha and Nooha, nurses who were all about my size, brought me their clothes, some of them brand-new. I kept them in a box in a dry place on the shelves in my new 'bedroom' in the operating-theatre.

Dry shoes were shared, worn by anyone who needed to

go out of the relatively dry operating-theatre. Fatme, a striking black-haired girl with huge dark eyes, gave me her beautiful white cotton scarf to keep me warm. The Palestinians are not at all possessive at the best of times, parting with personal belongings very readily. It is a custom that if you admire something you are given it, and I had to be very careful with my compliments.

Adham, the elder brother of Jihad, came to visit me from time to time, overcoming his dislike of hospitals. He would bring me *manaish*, a dough base a bit like a pizza, garnished either with *zatar* (thyme), or *haar* (onions and paprika). Souhar often brought *manaish* for the doctors, cooked by her mother, and her brother Feraz took pieces to Ben and Susie. Many people gave me cigarettes and I was smoking too much.

Lights were improvised for the hospital. All the batteries were removed from the cars in the camp along with their sidelights and headlight bulbs, and these were strung up around the hospital. When the generator was running the batteries were recharged.

The hospital was still taking a regular heavy battering. One afternoon I was sitting quietly in the operating-theatre when suddenly there was an earsplitting explosion as a bomb thundered against the outside wall and I felt the thud of the blast. I jumped to my feet to go to the emergency room, hearing people screaming and running for cover. As I staggered towards the door I was jolted by a second and third blast. It was like a dream in which you desperately try to run but seem to be moving very slowly. There were bright red flashes as more shells exploded. The building shook and my knees began to tremble.

I pushed past people crying in the dark corridor and cowered against Hassan as another bomb crashed into the wall right next to us. He put a comforting arm around me and whispered, 'Don't be afraid.' His words gave me strength and I struggled into the emergency room where people were coughing in the smoke and blowing the black soot out of their noses. Incredibly, no one was injured.

I had a slight cold and a couple of days later I had just finished the ward round on the first floor when a large rocket exploded right outside, only about three metres away from where I was standing. I felt slight pain and went completely deaf in my left ear. Later, I asked Ben to look in it and he saw a dark blot on the eardrum, probably blood. The ache continued and I was deaf for several days. I assumed it had ruptured my eardrum as I had seen happen to several bomb-blast victims. The hearing gradually recovered; at first sounds were echoey, like the noises in an indoor swimming-pool, but after two to three weeks it returned to normal.

A new problem was the burial of the dead, an impossible task during the shelling. At times the fridges, with room supposedly only for 6 bodies, became overloaded, with as many as 10–15 bodies. These were then buried all at once.

During one of these mass burials, in the cemetery at the edge of the camp, one of the hospital porters was killed. The man, Ibrahim, was standing in an exposed place. A friend shouted a warning, but too late. A shot rang out and Ibrahim fell on his face in the sand. He arrived dead at the hospital, shot through the neck. After this, the dead were buried in shallow temporary graves close to the hospital, in a place sheltered from gunfire.

The strain was beginning to tell on the young men. Many of them had been cooped up inside Bourj for a year and a half, not daring to go out after the first Camp War. Now they were seeing their friends and relations die and won-dering who would be next. All the while, they were doing long shifts at the front line shooting men who had previously been their allies. A few of the young fighters, I was told, smoked hashish, although it was generally frowned upon; others were taking Valium and other tranquillisers. Occasion-ally they came to Ben or to the hospital with stories about nervous mothers or sisters unable to sleep, or simply asking directly for tranquillisers. We tried to dispense as few as possible, only treating the genuinely disturbed.

Although some Arab governments had condemned the Camp War, the only ones really making serious efforts to find a solution to the conflict were the Iranians. I believe their reasons were twofold. They wanted to attract the many disaffected Amal militiamen who disagreed with the Camp War to the ranks of Hezbollah, who also disapproved of the fighting. But I think the Iranians also felt a genuine sympathy for the plight of the Palestinians beleaguered in the camps. A delegation, including the Iranian consul, went into Rashidiye on 10 December and refused to come out until the siege was lifted; they even went on hunger-strike.

Since the Palestinian militia had taken Magdoushe, the Camp War had been more prominent in the news and that day, on the BBC World Service, Gerald Butt reported that trucks of food and ambulances were allowed into Rashidiye which had been besieged for 'several weeks'. We were incensed.

'Several weeks', I thought. 'I bet he's never been under siege, otherwise he would know that there is a big difference between "several weeks" and two and a half months.' Our joy that relief had been given to Rashidiye lasted until the next day when Dr Mounir told us bitterly that the trucks had brought only rotten potatoes and onions. The food and medicines had been removed and the ambulances allowed to take out only the bodies of three dead Amal militiamen.

The Iranian plan involved an immediate ceasefire, the withdrawal of the Palestinians from Magdoushe and the lifting of the sieges. Amal, however, were insisting that the Palestinians withdraw first, while the Palestinians wanted the sieges lifted first, not trusting Amal to keep to the plan once they were back in command of Magdoushe. It was stalemate.

We began to see evidence of exhaustion in the nurses again. They resorted again to their drip bags, and even Dr

Nader succumbed and needed to be revived with an 'infusion'.

I too was tired, operating for hours and hours and looking after the wounded day after day. During Ben's evening visits, if I was not operating, we used to go and sit upstairs in my room on the sofa and drink hot chocolate made with milk-powder and cocoa.

When all my candles ran out, Ben brought home-made ones. A friend showed him how to melt cooking fat and pour it into little coffee cups with a gauze wick and Ben modified it by supporting the wick around a piece of wire. It burned very well and was better than the alternative made from 'fuel' in a Pepsi bottle with a wick through the top. These gave off a filthy black smoke. At the same time my Camping Gaz stove ran out of gas, and we had to heat the water by lighting spirit poured over cotton wool on the stone floor.

Ben and I shared our experiences of the day and dreamed up stories to tell each other about the holiday we would have after the war was over. One night I told Ben it would be in Venice. As a child I had visited the city with its silent canals and grand old palaces full of Renaissance art. Another night it was Egypt and Ben told me about the treasures in the Valley of the Kings. Or perhaps we would just go walking in the wild mountains of Scotland.

We tried to be discreet about our relationship, but it was not easy. Um Gemal was a warm-hearted, smiling forty-year-old woman who worked as a cleaner in the operating-theatre. Her husband was living outside the camp in Mar Elias so she brought her young child to work at the hospital with her. Shammes, which means 'sunshine', was a curious, pretty six-year-old who was very taken with Ben. We were trying to be discreet about Ben visiting me, but it was hopeless. Shammes asked me loudly almost every day: 'Is Ben coming tonight to see you?' or 'Are you getting married?' Sometimes she would run in and tell me, 'I've seen Ben,' and she would often follow us up to my room and drink hot chocolate with us. Um Gemal told her to be quiet, but it didn't make any difference.

The three patients who were in the hospital at the start of the war were moved down into the shelter where they occupied a small room three metres square. The young Shiite girl with polio deformities was doing well after removal of her plasters but the half-Syrian girl with two broken legs was depressed and Hannes often sat with her and they discussed the Bible. The operation on the ancient white-haired lady was supposed to immobilise her previously straight arm into a half-flexed position, so she could use it by moving the shoulder. But after we took off the plaster she simply started bending the arm and although the elbow was an awful shape it had good movement and she was even able to comb her hair.

Very deaf, confused and slightly senile, she thought Hannes was her grandson and I heard him shouting in her ear every day 'No, not Mohammed. Hannes, Hannes!' She knew nothing of the Amal militia and thought it was the Israelis who were attacking us. One day one of the young boys in the hospital asked her for a cup of tea. The deaf old lady said, 'I'll give you a cup of tea,' and threw her plastic beaker of tea all over him. Though not really knowing where she was now, she could still tell stories quite coherently about her earlier life in Palestine and the trouble all her sons had given her. The mother of the Shiite girl took care of all three of them.

On 18 December I heard on the radio that Nabila Breir, the woman at UNICEF in charge of Palestinian affairs, had been murdered. It was a brutal, savage act, even by Beirut standards. She had been machine-gunned to death in her car in Mar Elias street. Her only crime was that she was doing her job well, as she always did, providing aid and shelter for Palestinians, as well as poor Shiites and other deprived groups. It was one of the first times a woman had been killed in such a way and her death left me feeling empty and frightened. Obviously, from now on, women and civilians working for the relief agencies were also targets. I began to wonder whether I would get out of Bourj al Barajneh alive.

Towards the end of December, living conditions became extremely harsh, and still there was no respite from the daily shelling and shooting. Hundreds of families had been confined to crowded underground shelters or small ground-floor rooms for two months, the women only venturing out for the hazardous trip to fetch water from the taps in the alleys near the edges of the camp.

The underground shelters had no windows, sanitation or lighting. Susie visited patients in the shelters and said the stench was unbearable. Scabies and lice were completely out of control and there was not enough medicine to make any impact on them.

Little Ziad, a cheeky five-year-old urchin with a turned-up nose who was always begging for money, had moved in with his grandmother and his brothers and sisters to the hospital foyer, setting up camp at the bottom of a flight of stairs. One day he called to me, 'Doctora Pauline, Doctora Pauline. Look. I've got red spots.' He lifted up his jumper to show me. 'I've got those,' said a brother, pushing him aside. They all had scabies. I gave them a bottle of Benzyl Benzoate and explained how to use it, but it was stupid of me. They were supposed to shower, apply the medicine, shower and repeat the application after 12 hours and also wash their clothes. With only enough water to drink, it was a waste of the medicine.

'The garbage piles,' Ben told me one day, 'are becoming huge.' They were overflowing from their normal places and piling up in the squares and on the sites of destroyed houses. There were rats everywhere, but luckily, as it was winter, there were no flies or maggots.

One afternoon an old woman was brought into the

hospital. Bedridden from a previous stroke, and unable to summon help, she had lain in bed for three successive nights while rats had eaten away her toes. Eventually her family had rescued her during a lull in the fighting. The foot was badly infected and she was very ill. Despite our treatment with drip fluid antibiotics, she died 10 days later.

Generally the people of the camp maintained a high moral code, but there were some aberrations. A bit of thieving went on. Adnan, an illiterate man of 26, employed by the hospital as a messenger boy and porter, was a thief I knew of old. People warned me early on, 'Be careful of your things. Adnan is a thief.' But he was very amiable and his thieving was very obvious. He sometimes came into my room and, after looking round, slipped a cigarette lighter or a pen into his pocket. If I saw him, he would put them back at once. But others were helping themselves to torches, batteries and radios and occasionally stealing useful things from abandoned homes.

One who got caught was the sheikh's teenage son. The poor sheikh was so ashamed and mortified that he thought he ought to make an example of his son and threatened the boy with the ancient punishment of cutting off his hand. Everyone was horrified and the camp committee told him: 'No, no, no. You can't do that. Let us deal with it.' They put him under house arrest for a few days somewhere in the camp and then let him go. I was very glad; I had enough work without dealing with amputated hands.

At this time I heard news of one of my former patients. Abul Feda, the young man shot in the arm in the summer war, the one who had cried, 'My arm hurts,' all the time, was shot through the heart and killed. He had jumped out into the road and immobilised a tank with a rocket-propelled grenade before he was gunned down. His death saddened me. I had thought about him often, and now he was dead. There was something particularly awful about treating a patient, then seeing him brought back dead.

143

Two days later, the brother of Fadi, the boy so seriously wounded on the same day as Abul Feda in the summer war, was shot through the abdomen with an M-16 rifle. He looked incredibly like his brother and had 'Fadi' tattooed on his chest. His wound was in almost exactly the same place as Fadi's, but this time the bullet did not go into his chest. I helped Dr Mounir operate on him. He lost a kidney and his spleen and there was a lot of damaged bowel but he survived after a long recovery period.

Life in the hospital became gradually more difficult but we adapted to each new problem as it arose. The third floor collapsed and looking out of my window I could see pieces of mangled metal and a section of wall hanging precariously over the edge. The water tank had been totally destroyed and there was no running water in the hospital after mid-December. Plumbers at the hospital managed to seal off most of the pipes and partly stem the cascade of water from the roof, fixing up a smaller tank inside the building on the first floor above the foyer where water could be collected from a tap.

Cigarettes were becoming scarce. Our supply of coffee ran out. I had given all my coffee to Nooha, who thrived on coffee and disliked tea, but now it was all finished. Our meals had become insipid and boring. Apart from occasional plates of food brought by friends or evening snacks from Ben, like pieces of bread fried in icing sugar, I was eating a monotonous daily diet of boiled rice, cracked wheat and lentils. Occasionally we livened up the rice with tinned pilchards but such treats were scarce. Hassan brought a bottle of tomato ketchup from home and I applied it to almost everything I ate. In the evenings, Ben and I no longer discussed our holidays; the topic of conversation now was our favourite dishes and which restaurants we would eat in after the war. We were not alone in this. Everywhere I went I could hear people saying, 'Oh, do you know what I would like to eat now . . . ?'

Late one evening a group of about 10 of us were sitting around in the operating-theatre in the half light of a Pepsi-bottle lamp when Dr Aissam, the obstetrician, said to Dr Rede, 'Tell us some food stories.' We all sat transfixed with our mouths and taste-buds tingling while Dr Rede recounted the flavourful dishes he had eaten in Romania as a medical student.

I reckoned we were all becoming vitamin C deficient. My toothpaste ran out and I was using a local brand which did not contain fluoride; I became rather obsessed that, with the lack of vitamin C and fluoride, my teeth might fall out.

We were also running short of fuel. Stocks of diesel for the generators were almost exhausted and we ran the power only for emergencies. There was a little unrefined fuel in the camp, but it was dirty and clogged up the generators. The mechanic, Abu Sami, who worked wonders in keeping them going, was not optimistic that they would hold out for much longer than 10 days. Daytime was perpetual twilight and night-time was pitch-dark. I had given away one torch and the batteries in the other were finally flat after repeated recharging. I learned to live in the dark. I counted the stairs between the operating-theatre and my room, not forgetting the low brick dam at the top of the stairs and I put my key in a place on my key-ring where I could find it easily by touch alone. On several occasions I bumped into people who were also feeling their way around in the darkness.

I spent all my time in the hospital. In the past two months I had only been out of the building three or four times. As I noted in my diary: 'My world has become very small.' Apart from morning rounds to the patients' rooms and tending to them during the day, I spent my whole time in five rooms: the operating-theatre, the emergency room, the X-ray room, the doctors' room and my room.

The hours in the cold darkness, when we were not operating or working frantically in the emergency room, were monotonous and dreary. Our spirits got very low at times. Dr Rede became depressed and uncommunicative and I could tell he was missing Erica. Dr Mounir remained cheerful. In 1982 he had been arrested by the Israelis and taken from the clinic in which he was working in the South to prison in Israel. They kept him there for nine months, during which time he was occasionally maltreated and humiliated. In prison, he said, he had learned ways to keep his spirits up. He prepared little treats for us by squirrelling away titbits of food in a trunk in the doctors' room during the day to give us a midnight feast. Although the 'feast' was often only a few scraps of bread, a handful of olives and a small plate of watery hummus between four or five of us, it was something to look forward to.

Hannes and Nooha whiled away the hours discussing religion and marriage. Hannes was a devout Christian, always offering a silent prayer before he ate, and Nooha was a devout Muslim. Neither was a proselytiser, but they would spend hours discussing the details of the scriptures and the Koran, and whether Jesus was just a prophet or the son of God. Many of these conversations would end with Nooha saying, 'Well, I could marry you but you would have to convert to Islam,' to which Hannes would reply, 'Well, *I* could marry *you* but you would have to convert to Christianity.' Listening to these endless debates, I was struck not by the differences but by the similarities between the two religions.

As Christmas approached, we four foreign workers began to make preparations. With Susie's paintbox, a felt-tipped pen and cardboard ripped off the back of prescription pads, I made Christmas cards. For the Palestinians, the operating-theatre staff and the hospital staff I painted Christmas trees in the colours of the Palestinian flag. For Hannes I did a silhouette of the Madonna and child. Susie got a Christmas tree. For Ben and the doctors I drew a picture of Haifa Hospital, the Christmas star shining above it, and bombs

falling from the sky. Susie made an Advent calender and
Christmas decorations. Hannes made cards with quotations
from the Bible, while Ben gathered food for a feast.

There would be no presents this Christmas. We had
nothing to give.

Chapter 12

Christmas Day dawned like any other. My first task on Christmas morning was to assist Dr Aissam in a difficult Caesarean section. The baby, a girl, was born at 8.30 a.m.

I joined the ward round and handed out the Christmas cards I had made. People wished us a happy Christmas and Nooha pinned up the cards I'd made for the operating-theatre staff on the notice board in the ante-room where the operating lists used to be posted.

Then I went down to the hospital shelter to look at the amputation stump of a young man who had lost his leg. We tried to make it a rule that the rooms be cleared of family and visitors for dressings as most patients did not want their wounds and bodies exposed to an audience. As they slowly drifted out, Imad, the patient, got impatient, barking out, 'Come on, come on, get out, all of you!'

In the next bed was Sofaa, a young man who had been almost blinded by sand-blast. Both eyes bandaged, he called out to his friends, 'Hey, wait. Where are you going? What's happening?'

'I'm having my dressing done and they have to go out,' said Imad indignantly.

Sofaa protested and they started arguing. Eventually Imad shouted, 'You shut up or I'll cut your head off!'

'You shut up or I'll cut your leg off!' yelled Sofaa.

Everyone became quiet.

'Er, does he know you've lost a leg?' I whispered to Imad in Arabic.

'Yes, he does,' retorted Imad, scowling at Sofaa. 'He wants to cut the other one off!'

Then to my relief they both laughed sheepishly.

The morning passed quietly with only a few shrapnel wounds to treat. I was about to go down to the clinic for Ben's Christmas dinner when I heard the sound of running feet. There was panic in the corridor, then two young men were rushed into the emergency room. One was already dead from terrible shrapnel wounds. The other had a severe head injury with multiple skull fractures and three large pieces of shrapnel deep in the brain.

After the survival of the first two patients who underwent neurosurgery, I had attempted another, more serious, case and had been totally unable to stop the bleeding. Nooha told me, 'I've seen many like this. Even in the most experienced hands, with all the special instruments, these cases are hopeless.' After that we decided to reserve our resources and efforts for those patients who were in a better condition, and used as a basic criterion that they must at least be breathing unassisted before the operation.

The man on Christmas Day could not breathe on his own. For two hours we ventilated him by hand, but every time we stopped he made no effort to breathe and apart from an increasingly faint heartbeat he showed no signs of life. After two hours we stopped ventilating him and he died.

His death cast a dark shadow over that Christmas Day and when I at last went down to the clinic in the evening it was at first a sombre gathering. Ben had collected together from neighbours a tin of Spam, some tomato paste, an onion and a piece of old cheese. With these unpromising ingredients he had made a spaghetti. It was so delicious, such a change from plain boiled rice, that our spirits rose. One of the men had even secretly brought us a bottle of his home-made red wine in a plastic bottle, which he claimed was vintage, six years old. It too tasted very good.

Ben, Susie, Hannes and I sat around the blue wooden table, between the first-aid couches and the dressing trolley. We were in the small back room of the clinic with sandbags piled up against the windows. Susie had secured a precious candle for the occasion and its flickering light illuminated the table decorations she had made from pretty purple and silver lace. The clinic was dry, the company was good, and the food and wine warmed me up. It was a Christmas dinner I shall never forget.

When the meal was over, Ben walked with Hannes and me back up the hill to the hospital. He still had a torch but its beam was dim and we picked our way carefully along the narrow paths between the houses, trying not to step into the open drains or fall over the water-pipes and piles of bricks and rubble. We could hear rats scrabbling in the rubbish piles. It was very eerie, the quiet broken by the whack of snipers bullets hitting the exposed buildings above us. All the time we were trying to hurry, nerves tingling, knowing that any minute a bomb might land and blow us to pieces.

'Ben,' I said, when we at last reached the safety of the hospital, 'I don't know how you can do this every day.' He made the journey from the hospital regularly, bringing gauze to be sterilised for his clinic.

'I recite to myself "*Bism Allah rahman wa rahim*" which means "In the name of God the merciful", and then I run like hell,' he said with a laugh. 'Once, I had to jump into a doorway when a shell landed about 20 metres in front of me, but so far I've only once fallen flat on my face in the dirt.'

The couple of days following Christmas were relatively quiet but the news from Chatila was not good. There were rumours that the hospital complex had been hit and that tanks were pounding the camp at close range, levelling the houses at the perimeter and working their way inwards. The people had withdrawn to the centre of the camp and were staying underground as much as possible.

We also heard news of a fresh Iranian offensive against Iraq in the Gulf War. Both the Iranians and the Iraqis claimed that thousands of the other's soldiers had been killed. I thought about our hospital and how difficult we found it to cope with 15–20 wounded people at once. How could they possibly deal with thousands? There wasn't a system in the world that could cope with those numbers and the battleground was a vast watery swamp. Many must just lie there and die.

On 29 December, the BBC World Service reported that Nabih Berri had announced a 'Goodwill ceasefire' for the New Year. The next day showed what his idea of a ceasefire was like. That morning, Hassan's sister was shot in the arm while collecting water. The corrugated iron screen erected to protect the tap from snipers had blown down in a gale in the night and she hadn't realised. A nine-year-old boy was shot in the head and killed. Then, little Bilal was wounded by a sniper's bullet, paralysing him from the waist down for ever. That night I wrote in my diary: 'So much for Berri's ceasefire.'

On New Year's Eve, Ben came up to the hospital in the evening and the operating-theatre staff prepared a meal. Nooha spread a grey blanket on the floor, then we all sat around a big aluminium tray with plates of hummus, olives and corned beef and the last of the potatoes, fried. We ate with scraps of stale bread, also the last. When we had finished, the doctors and nurses gathered at midnight and we went round all the patients wishing them a happy New Year.

Ben and I crept up to my room to share a miniature of cherry brandy, a present from a man who lived nearby, but this particular New Year's Day felt more like an occasion for mourning than rejoicing.

The first day of the New Year brought no good news. There was still stalemate over Magdoushe, the fighting continued unabated there and the siege of Bourj, now in its third month, remained as tight as ever. Stocks in the camp were virtually exhausted. Almost all daily necessities had run out in the camp and many things were scarce.

There was no milk-powder for babies. For some time the hospital and Susie had been distributing tins of special milk to families with a baby under six months old. The baby had to be produced as evidence before a precious tin was handed over. All mothers were encouraged to breast-feed, but with the psychological stress of the war, the worsening living conditions and the poor diet, many mothers were providing insufficient milk and babies needed powdered milk. When that ran out they were given tea and water with sugar.

There was no flour left in Bourj al Barajneh, and consequently no bread. In the hospital, food was rationed for both patients and staff. We had breakfast, usually rice pudding, and one meal in the evening, usually rice, cracked wheat, lentils or the dreaded safari meat, poor quality tinned corned beef which clogged in the mouth and was very unappetising. There were jokes that if this situation carried on much longer we would be eating cats and dogs.

One day, some of us were gathered around the entrance to the emergency room when a young man walked past with a little hairy mongrel dog on a lead. One of the young men watching smacked his lips and called out, 'Yum, yum, yum!'

'Keep feeding it, keep feeding it,' shouted another.

People went on donating blood for the wounded, of course, but with their inadequate diet it was increasingly difficult for them to make up the deficit.

I felt sorry for one patient. He had been shot in the chest in early December and although he recovered slowly, for weeks afterwards he got pain in his mid-lower chest if he ate anything solid, so I kept him on slops and custard. On one of those days he handed me a packet of biscuits and said, 'I can't eat these. You have them.' Now, laughing ruefully, he reminded me of the gift and said, 'Now I can eat biscuits again, there aren't any.' Then he repeated his favourite saying, 'Bas Allah kebir', which means 'But God is supreme'.

The pharmacists gave us daily reports on the stocks of

medicine. Some were very low and we made a policy of restricting various medicines to serious cases, using alternatives if possible. Dr Rede asked the pharmacists to keep us constantly aware of what we had left. The UNRWA out-patient clinic near the hospital, which had been closed since the beginning of the fighting, as it had in the summer war, was opened up by the UNRWA representative living in the camp. He cleared out all its medicines and brought them to the hospital. The lack of pain-killing tablets was a big problem and we often had to make do with anti-inflammatories and tranquillisers.

In early January, our biggest crisis, that of fuel, was temporarily alleviated. During the previous three weeks a man had dug a 40-metre tunnel under the road to a petrol station on the opposite corner of the street across from the bottom of the camp. So as not to be heard, he dug by hand, carefully lifting out rocks. A man in the camp, who had worked at the garage, provided him with plans showing the whereabouts of the underground tanks. When they tapped the tanks they were found to be almost full. For days, many people in the camps took turns to run up the hill to us with five-gallon plastic containers of diesel. It was not possible to use a motor to pump out the diesel because of the noise; those who went into the tunnel told of hearing Amal militiamen walking and talking overhead. In total, 4,000 gallons were siphoned out of the tanks, enough to run the generators 12 hours a day for six weeks. It was a tremendous boost to our morale. We could have light for four hours at a stretch without worrying about the fuel supply.

Hassan brought his television set to the hospital and set it up at one end of the operating-theatre ante-room, trailing the aerial out of the window through a hole between the sandbags and attaching it to a metal pipe. At night, if we were not working, he switched it on. One network was showing a weekly series of old American films and we escaped into *Rebel Without a Cause* and a disaster movie about a plane crashing into the Potomac River in Washington D.C.

One evening a television news broadcast showed an American attempt to break the record for the longest sandwich in the world. We watched giggling with disbelief as teams of people piled salami, cheese, salmon, lettuce, tomato, pickle, mayonnaise and God knows what else into a 200-metre-long sandwich!

By now I had begun to feel the grip of hunger in my stomach. It didn't rumble, but it felt empty all the time and there was a sharp pain which was only partly relieved by eating. From now on, the pain never really went away. I knew everyone else was feeling it too and we never spoke about it.

On 9 January, I was feeling very low. The evening was quiet so I went down to the clinic for an hour with Ben. He heated up some left-over tinned fish with rice. As I started to eat, uncontrolled tears of relief ran down my cheeks and dripped on to the plate and I had to admit to Ben how hungry I'd been.

News from Chatila was disturbing: three cases of typhoid. They did not have a clean water-supply and were collecting rainwater to drink. Outside the camps, there were clashes. Beirut airport was bombed from the east and a plane set on fire. The Iranian peace plan had come to nothing and now people were pinning their hopes on a meeting of the Arab League foreign ministers, due to be held on 26 January in Tunis.

I discovered I had head lice.

In the middle of January the bombardment of the camp became more sporadic. Our work reflected the change. Most of our patients now were the victims of snipers, usually with lethal high-velocity M-16 wounds. People were shot as they came out into the alleys, no longer able to bear the nightmare conditions in the shelters. Knowing we were still working very hard, families who still had some food left occasionally invited to lunch the doctors and those who had no family in the camp. Often no more than tinned spaghetti, hummus, olives and bulgar wheat mixed up with paprika, these meals were like feasts to us, a welcome change from the monotony of the hospital diet.

My life continued to revolve around the operating-theatre, the emergency room and the doctors' room. Dr Mounir, Dr Nader and Dr Dergham lived in the doctors' room with an adjoining shower and toilet which now could only be flushed by pouring in water from a plastic jug. Every day I went in there, the beds were in a slightly different position as the three of them moved in a circuit around the room, trying in vain to avoid the water dripping every few seconds from the ceiling and forming the inevitable pool on the floor.

Greeny-brown mould was growing on the pale grey walls here, as everywhere else, and protruding in through the outer wall were the ends of the rusting iron struts which supported the fortification wall. On them hung two towels and a pair of Dr Dergham's underpants. A dark blue metal trunk, which belonged to Ben and was now used only occasionally by Dr Mounir as a food-hiding place, a wooden chair and a small plastic-and-chrome table were the only other pieces of furniture. A 1986 calender, on which Dr Rede had for two months circled the dates on which he anticipated that the war would end, was now blank, its face turned to the wall.

Cigarettes were extremely scarce. We got a daily ration of two from Dr Rede, who was put in charge of the cigarette supply because he did not smoke, and sometimes another one as a gift from people in the camp. I smoked mine a half at a time, and tried to make them last through the day. Although the enforced cutting down on smoking was better for our health, these were not ideal circumstances in which to give up. One day a friend brought a whole Marlboro cigarette, his favourite, to Dr Nader. Dr Nader, tall, dark and now thin in his blood-stained beige track suit, lit it, leaned back in his chair and said slowly in a John Wayne accent, 'Welcome to Marlboro country.' We laughed and laughed as he passed around the cigarette. It became Dr Nader's catch-phrase. Even when, having completely exhausted the supply of real cigarettes, we were reduced to sharing one made out of dry tea-leaves rolled in paper tied up with cotton, he still said it.

Dr Mounir, if he had no cigarettes, would sing, 'I, I who have nothing', hoping to prompt someone to light one and share it. If he had a cigarette, he would change the song to 'I, I who have something', moisten his fingers on his tongue, reach inside his jumper to his breast-pocket and then pull it out with a theatrical gesture. Sometimes, to tease us, he would go through this ritual but only pull out his prayer beads.

Dr Mounir was generally extroverted and could be fierce when he was angry, but in quiet moments he admitted that he missed his two children dreadfully and worried about their safety and that of his wife in Akka Hospital.

Two and a half weeks after his injury, little Bilal was cheerfully recovering and playing with toys, despite his paralysis. Then he had a relapse. One of his lungs collapsed and I had to put in another drain. Even then, he did not make much of a fuss. The little boy was becoming a special favourite of mine. I went to see him every day. He'd play with my stethoscope, listening to his own chest. Ben brought him some toys from the camp and the hospital staff gave him titbits.

Dr Rede was running a chess school. Having long ago got over missing the international tournament in the Gulf at which he was supposed to represent Palestine the previous autumn, he decided to hold his own. No one could beat him consistently, although Dr Mounir managed once or twice. Hannes played regularly with Adnan, the anaesthetic-technician. Neither was particularly good but

Adnan claimed that Hannes played without any scheme but could still win, which infuritated him. Ben and I began to play. We were both hopeless, but luckily we were equally hopeless, so the scores were about even. The outside world seemed a long, long way away.

Money now had no value in the camp. There was nothing to buy. News of the collapse of the Lebanese pound meant little. It seemed as if it had nothing to do with us.

The hospital foyer was a madhouse. The children of the families living there had been cooped up for nearly three months and sometimes ran excitedly around in the corridors. We were still receiving seriously wounded people every day and they got in our way. The shelter was full to overflowing with convalescing patients, some of whom under normal circumstances could have been discharged but whose homes were partly or completely destroyed. The camp committee found places in a few 'safe' houses and now that the bombardments were not quite so intense or frequent, with some persuasion, most of the people moved out from the hospital.

By the end of the second week of January the situation in the camp was critical. So many vital items had run out: batteries, candles, matches, cigarettes, gas for cooking. The women in the hospital kitchen, like most people in the camp, were now cooking and heating water for washing the operating-theatre linen on wood fires built from bricks and a metal grill, just outside the kitchen opposite my room. The water still had to be collected daily, at great risk, from the outside taps.

For my birthday on 19 January, Ben brought me a present, a 'siege-survival kit', of socks, soap, toothpaste *with* fluoride, two candles and a whole packet of cigarettes! It was the best present I'd ever had.

The medicine crisis was worsening all the time. Painkillers and some antibiotics had to be severely rationed. We were reusing washed-out crepe bandages which rapidly lost their capacity to stretch and could not be guaranteeed to be clean.

Conventional anaesthetic gases such as nitrous oxide were finished and there were only two cylinders of oxygen remaining. Adnan, the anaesthetic-technician, had to use his considerable ingenuity to improvise ways of keeping asleep patients who were undergoing major surgery. He used a cocktail of intravenous sedatives and relaxants while ventilating them on air.

One evening, a young man asked me in Arabic, provocatively, 'If Nabih Berri came in wounded now, would you treat him?' 'Yes, I would,' I replied in Arabic. 'As a doctor, I would treat anyone who needed it. But,' I continued, 'I would have to say to him, "Mr Berri, you need an operation but I'm afraid we don't have any anaesthetics, so we have to do it without. OK?"' The young man laughed.

However, the most serious problem was the lack of food. Bourj al Barajneh was being starved into submission. Every day now we were seeing health problems related to malnutrition. Children and babies in particular were affected, presented in increasing numbers at the GP clinics with skin diseases and infections which would not heal up, mouth ulcers, weight loss, malaise, chronic coughs and colds, nausea and diarrhoea, or constipation.

At the hospital we were seeing wounds which stubbornly refused to heal and became readily infected. We dispensed the limited supply of multivitamin tablets and syrup sparingly. We were all losing weight slowly. Even Dr Dergham's previously rotund figure was becoming trim and when we commented he told us that for some time he had been taking half his meagre one meal a day to a poor family living nearby whose children were hungry. People were still very generous with food. Adham, the brother of Jihad, still sometimes brought me plates of rice and olives. I protested that I did not want to take his family's food.

'While I have a little, I will bring you a little,' he told me. 'When we have nothing, *then* I will bring you nothing.'

When food was brought to the operating-theatre, Nooha would call, '*Tefaddal, tefaddal,*' or, 'Come and eat, come and eat.' Amar, a medical student, a voluntary anaesthetic assistant, shared food brought by his mother. He also saved his cigarettes to smoke with me. I did not yearn for fancy food any more. Conversations about food had ceased completely.

The communal kitchen feeding Ben and Susie closed and they collected their one meal a day from the hospital. A gentle, quiet-spoken woman living near the clinic brought them a share of the food she cooked for the day for her family.

I found that work tired me more quickly. I became easily irritated by people who came with petty, mundane problems, but then always felt guilty afterwards.

The weather was still bitterly cold. From the moment I got up in the morning, the icy cold would begin at my toes and creep up my legs until after an hour they were numb from the knee down for the rest of the day. I saw three children with mottled blue blistered toes, a form of frostbite. Susie was seized by fits of coughing, day and night.

By now the Camp War had disappeared from the news and we felt cut off and forgotten. Most news broadcasts concentrated on the new wave of kidnappings in West Beirut. A French TV/radio journalist was taken on 13 January and, soon after, two West German businessmen, apparently as a bargaining counter for the release of Ali Hamadi, a Lebanese Shiite accused of the TWA hijacking in 1985 who was imprisoned in West Germany. Then, three Americans were kidnapped from the campus of the American University and Terry Waite, the Archbishop of Canterbury's special envoy, disappeared when he went alone to negotiate with the kidnappers. There was talk of direct Syrian intervention in West Beirut, but no concrete change.

The strain began to tell on some of us in the hospital and tempers flared.

The hospital generator was now the only source of electricity in the camp and political groups were running electricity lines from the hospital to their offices. If we were not operating, it was not a problem, but one day, when the generator cut out due to overload in the middle of an operation, Dr Rede went around the hospital ordering the removal of the lines and disconnecting them. Samir, the bossy, hot-tempered radiographer, objected. 'Put it back!' he shouted at Dr Rede when he pulled out the line running from his department. 'I'm responsible here.' Dr Rede refused and an argument ensued. It ended with Samir drawing his pistol and shooting around Dr Rede's feet.

I heard the sound of shooting inside the hospital and ran down to the emergency room. There I heard the story from the people milling around. Dr Rede had disappeared from the hospital, apparently unhurt. I could hardly believe what I heard and went to the X-ray room where I found Samir sitting on his camp-bed.

'Did you shoot at Dr Rede?' I asked, incredulously.

'Yes, I did!' roared the unrepentant Samir. 'I will kill him and anyone who stands with him!'

I knew that Dr Rede's actions were always for the common good and my control snapped. 'Well, you can kill me,' I yelled back, shaking with anger, 'because *I* stand with Dr Rede.' Then I stormed out of the room.

Dr Rede returned to the hospital with the chiefs of the camp committee. 'Six-gun' Samir had, of course, calmed down by then, but he was banished from the hospital, and the work in the X-ray department had to be done by his assistant.

Chapter 13

As we entered the last two weeks of January, it was obvious to everyone that we were now starving. Dr Rede sent out an appeal on the walkie-talkie to UNRWA on behalf of 'the Doctors of Haifa Hospital', telling them that we had run out of food and medicines and beseeching the combatants to agree to a ceasefire to allow supplies to be brought in.

From Mar Elias we heard that UNRWA were trying to negotiate with Amal to allow relief supplies into the camps, but of the appeal we heard nothing. Ben was not surprised. 'It's very sad,' he said, 'but nobody listens to the Palestinians. I've seen it before. The Palestinians are a problem the world wishes did not exist.'

Outside, the food problem in the camps was being denied and one report even said that there were no civilians in the camps, only PLO fighters! It wasn't true. Almost all the men fighting were civilians in normal times, and all had their families here with them. Only a few fighters had been brought in *after* the first Camp War to aid in the defence of the camps.

The actual situation in the camps was being hidden from the outside world by a veil of untruths. The Amal militia, having failed to take the camps by military force, were attempting to bludgeon them into submission by a war of attrition. And if that were to happen, if the camps capitulated, what everyone feared most was the prospect of ensuing massacre. There had been just such a massacre in 1976 after the defeat of Tel al Zatar. Some of the survivors were now living in Bourj. Dr Nader was one. He had been a seventeen-year-old boy when Tel al Zatar fell. His brother and his nephew were killed and his sister-in-law, a Swedish nurse, lost an arm.

Tel al Zatar was a Palestinian refugee camp in East Beirut. In 1976, at the start of the civil war, the Christian Phalangists were 'cleaning out' the Muslims from the suburbs of East Beirut, and Tel al Zatar camp was included in their sweep. The Phelangists, aided by the Syrians, surrounded the camp. 'The problem that defeated the camp,' Dr Nader explained, 'was the lack of water.'

The camp had no independent water-supply and, when people began to die of thirst, the inhabitants surrendered and agreed to evacuate. As the population left the camp, many were slaughtered, mostly the men, and 1,500 were killed on one day. Then the camp was bulldozed. A similar fate had befallen the mainly Shiite shanty town suburbs of Nabaa and Qarantina, the survivors fleeing to West Beirut. In revenge, the Muslims massacred 500 Christians in Damour, south of Beirut.

I had a copy of Helena Cobban's book *The Making of Modern Lebanon* and I read the paragraphs about Tel al Zatar. The parallels with the present siege of Bourj al Barajneh were frighteningly apparent.

Ben sometimes recalled the Sabra and Chatila massacre in 1982. He had been there, working in Gaza Hospital in Sabra, during the three days of slaughter. He had been unaware of what was happening until he and the other foreign health workers were ordered out of the hospital at gunpoint by the Phalangists. They were marched past the dead bodies littering the camp and groups of the inhabitants herded together. When they saw the foreigners the women tried to thrust their babies into their hands but were pushed back by the militiamen.

One of the health workers was a Palestinian male nurse. As the only Arab he was singled out and asked for his identity card. When the Phalangists saw that it was blue –

meaning he was a Palestinian – they hustled him behind a wall and shot him.

Ben and the others were ordered to remove their hospital clothes, then lined up with their backs to a wall. Facing ┼hem were six men pointing M-16 rifles. 'Oh God,' said one of the doctors, 'it's a firing squad.'

At this point an Israeli soldier who had been standing by, watching the massacre, decided to intervene. Ben and his colleagues were taken to Israeli headquarters.

It was a horrible irony. Israeli soldiers were colluding with a militia modelled on Hitler's Nazis.

I became increasingly terrified by the idea that the camp would be overrun and we would all be killed. I thought about it constantly and had nightmares at night. The hospital had been repeatedly bombed, women and children shot, wounded denied transfer to specialist units. Nabila Breir, the woman who worked for UNICEF, had been killed in the street and now the imminent starvation of the camp population was being concealed. Yes, the fear of a massacre was very real indeed.

On 23 January I wrote in my diary: 'Things have got worse. Before, I was missing home comforts, but, now it has become more serious, I don't. Food is running out in the camp and people are hungry. There is no milk, and no bread. I know I have become hungrier because the rice and bulgar wheat now tastes good. I do not long for other food any more. I had a terrible dream last night that 10 wounded came all at once but they were all dead with the flesh rotting off and most were skeletons. One was a friend and some had traumatic amputations. We were surrounded in the hospital and being shot at. We tried to escape through a small dark tunnel but the way was blocked by pigs falling on us. There is still no end in sight. Yesterday I smoked some tea. It wasn't bad. But despite everything I am in good spirits.'

That day I took Ben aside and said, 'I think we must

speak out and tell the truth about what is happening here. What do you think?' He agreed. We talked to Dr Rede. In view of the fate that had befallen Nabila Breir, we knew that to disclose our presence in the camp might be to expose us to risk from outside but we were not prepared to remain silent and see the camp squeezed into extinction.

'I think we should give our names so that there is no question of who is providing the information,' I said to Ben.

I wrote the declaration on some scrap paper and Ben took it to Susie to ask her opinion and to make any amendments. Hannes decided to remain anonymous. His mother was very nervous, he explained, and if she got to hear of his terrible predicament, it would be too much for her.

That afternoon, 23 January, Dr Rede sent out the following statement to Mar Elias on the walkie-talkie:

DECLARATION FROM FOREIGN HEALTH WORKERS IN BOURJ AL BARAJNEH REFUGEE CAMP

WE, AS FOREIGN HEALTH WORKERS LIVING AND WORKING IN BOURJ AL BARAJNEH REFUGEE CAMP, DECLARE THAT THE SITUATION IN THE CAMP IS CRITICAL AND CONDITIONS INHUMANE. THE CAMP HAS NOW BEEN UNDER SIEGE FOR MORE THAN 12 WEEKS AND WE AND THE 20,000 RESIDENTS ARE BEING SUBJECTED TO CONDITIONS OF DEPRIVATION AND MISERY. DRINKING-WATER IS THE MOST BASIC HUMAN NEED. MOST HOUSES DO NOT HAVE RUNNING DRINKING-WATER AND IT HAS TO BE COLLECTED DAILY FROM TAPS IN THE STREETS AND AT GREAT RISK OF PERSONAL SAFETY. SEVERAL WOMEN HAVE BEEN SHOT AND KILLED COLLECTING WATER FOR THEIR FAMILIES. FOOD STOCKS HAVE BEEN COMPLETELY DEPLETED. THERE IS NOW NO BABY-FOOD OR MILK AND BABIES ARE DRINKING TEA AND WATER. THERE IS NO FLOUR AND THEREFORE NO BREAD, NO FRESH FOOD SO PREGNANT WOMEN AND CHILDREN

ARE SUFFERING UNDERNOURISHMENT. PEOPLE ARE
EATING STALE FOOD AND SUFFERING VOMITING AND
DIARRHOEA. MANY FAMILIES NOW HAVE NO FOOD. IT IS
WINTER AND THE ELECTRICITY WAS CUT OFF FROM THE
CAMP TWO AND A HALF MONTHS AGO. PEOPLE ARE COLD
AND HAVE CHEST INFECTIONS. THERE ARE HUGE PILES OF
GARBAGE WHICH CANNOT BE CLEARED AND RATS ARE
THRIVING. ONE OLD LADY WHO WAS BEDRIDDEN WAS
UNABLE TO GET HELP WHEN HER FOOT WAS EATEN BY
RATS FOR THREE CONSECUTIVE NIGHTS, BEFORE SHE
WAS RESCUED. THE CONSTANT BOMBARDMENT OF THE
CAMP FORCES THE PEOPLE TO CROWD INTO POORLY
VENTILATED SHELTERS WITH NO SANITATION OR TO RISK
BEING BLOWN UP AT HOME. HUNDREDS OF CHILDREN
HAVE SCABIES AND MANY HAVE SEVERE SKIN INFECTIONS.
APPROXIMATELY 35 PER CENT OF HOMES IN BOURJ AL
BARAJNEH HAVE NOW BEEN DESTROYED. IN THE
HOSPITAL, MANY MEDICINES HAVE RUN OUT AND WE
HAVE NO MORE GAUZE. THE HOSPITAL BUILDING IS BEING
RENDERED UNSTABLE BY REPEATED SHELLING AND
PATIENTS AND NURSES HAVE BEEN INJURED BY SHRAPNEL.
WATER IS DRIPPING DOWN THE WALLS AND MOULD IS
GROWING IN EVERY ROOM.

WE DECLARE THESE CONDITIONS TO BE INHUMANE AND
ON HUMANITARIAN GROUNDS WE CALL FOR THE LIFTING
OF THE SIEGE AND THE ADMISSION OF FOOD AND MEDI-
CINES BY THE INTERNATIONAL RELIEF AGENCIES.

DR PAULINE CUTTING – BRITISH SURGEON
BEN ALOFS – DUTCH NURSE
SUSAN WIGHTON – SCOTTISH NURSE

We asked the doctor in charge at Mar Elias to circulate it
to UNRWA, the International Red Cross, foreign ambas-
sadors, our organisations at home and anyone else they saw
fit. It took quite a long time to transmit and several times

the frequency on the walkie-talkie had to be changed as intruders interfered with and jammed the transmission.

The following day, one of the nurses told me that our declaration had been read out on the news in Arabic. That was very good news. At least now, I thought, those outside the camp could not ignore the Palestinians. Specifically, I hoped the issue of the Palestinians would be urgently discussed at the meeting of Arab League foreign ministers in Tunis at the end of that week.

In fact, the Iran/Iraq war was the main item on the agenda; thousands were dying in the renewed offensive. But the Camp Wars in Lebanon were discussed and condemned. It was proposed that a multinational Arab force should be deployed around the camps to keep the warring parties apart. The idea was welcomed in Bourj al Barajneh. A Western multinational force had protected the camps in late 1982 after the massacres in Sabra and Chatila in September 1982 by the Phalangists. The Italian contingent stayed on around Bourj through 1983 and they were well loved by the Palestinians. Most homes in the camp had souvenir photos in their albums of their favourite Italian soldiers. But despite all the speech-making in Tunis, nothing happened. The siege went on.

There were rumours going round Bourj about behind-the-scenes negotiations at the conference. One was that Saudi Arabia was paying a large sum of money to Syria (one hundred million dollars was mentioned) to intervene and stop the war. But this remained a rumour and no official confirmation ever came.

In the camp, two mules were slaughtered and the meat distributed. Ben was rather sad as he had treated one of the mules for a shrapnel wound in September 1985. The generator mechanic brought Ben and me a plate of mule-meat chunks fried in a little garlic. It was not much but mouth-wateringly tasty. Ben and Susie were given the mule's food, a bag of bran, which Ben made into biscuits with a little sugar and water – not very nutritious, but filling.

People were eating what they could find and saving every scrap. Ben saw children searching the garbage for scraps of food and Ziad was seen cooking a rat. Many had diarrhoea and vomiting as a result of eating old contaminated food. Some young men made daring night-time sorties, creeping out over the sand-hills and across the airport road to a rubbish dump where a Lebanese friend had agreed, after contact on the walkie-talkie, to leave some food. But on the second attempt they were ambushed. One managed to get back into the camp and told us that the first man who crossed the road was met by a hail of bullets and wounded. He called back, 'Don't come out! It's a trap!'

Another man went to try to pick him up but he too was shot. He spoke a few words, then was silent. The third tried to save his friends but was shot in the chest before he could get clear. He scrambled back into the camp. His wound was serious, but he would live. He was inconsolable and brooded about the fate of his friends, one dead and the other wounded, almost certain to be killed.

Other men were more successful, sneaking in at night from outside the camp dressed in Lebanese Army 6th Brigade uniforms. But they could only bring in what they could carry and of course they couldn't leave, becoming yet another mouth to feed. That week I saw a nine-year-old child in the emergency room who had fainted twice from hunger.

The Iranians and Hezbollah were still making efforts to provide relief for the camps and had succeeded in a small way in Rashidiye. On 28 January they managed to gain entry to Bourj with six cars and evacuated 12 patients. Having been isolated for so long, their entry was a major event. Hundreds of people came rushing from all over the camp. This time I was determined not to be shut in my room. I wanted to see them.

There were 12 or so men with thick black beards, dressed in dark green fatigues, but what struck me about them was that, plump, pink-cheeked and energetic, they were so healthy. The people from the camp who came out to watch were like a race of zombies; filthy, pale, slow-moving, thin and dark-eyed, they stood in the mud and garbage with hunched shoulders. Some managed to siphon the petrol out of the cars for the hospital. Then the Hezbollah men left; they had been perfectly courteous and had taken little notice of me.

They had tried to get a truck full of tins of powdered milk in, but the driver was shot as he drove towards the camp and the truck was left stranded in the no man's land just outside the perimeter. That night, three boys crept out to it, stealthily removed tins of milk and brought them in. For several days we drank milk again, but it was soon finished.

The next day a 39-year-old women was shot in both legs and an arm when she ventured into an exposed place while picking grass at the edge of the camp to feed her children. She herself had not eaten anything for three days. A twelve-year-old boy I knew was shot in the head and killed, similarly picking grass to eat. A whole family, mother, father and six children were treated in the hospital one evening, vomiting violently after cooking and eating a stew of weeds.

On 30 January, the Palestinians capitulated and withdrew from Magdoushe. At last, we thought, this siege will be lifted. First they handed their positions over to the Nasserites, the Sunni militia who controlled Saida, and to Hezbollah. Three days later those groups handed them back to Amal. It was rumoured that the Hezbollah commander had wanted to knock down an imposing statue of the Virgin Mary on the hill of Magdoushe on the grounds that it offended Islam, but the Palestinian commander refused, saying that, after all, Mary was a Palestinian.

But still nothing changed.

There was no food left in the camp. In the GP out-patient clinics, the problems of malnutrition were compounded by acute starvation. People were losing weight rapidly and complained of headaches, abdominal pain, nausea, weakness, fainting and a tendency to collapse. Wounds which had healed, reopened.

One morning, two young men stopped me in the hospital corridor and asked me, confidentially, whether eating the flesh of cats would do them any harm. I said, 'No, it would not,' but I guessed by their manner that they had already eaten some. When I told the other doctors, they said they had received similar queries about cats, dogs and frogs.

The joking had become reality. People were not speaking very openly about it but eating cats and dogs had become fairly widespread. Other doctors told me that the people felt ashamed and degraded by the act.

Some young men maintained their bravado and the banter changed to jokes about eating each other. One young man, who was married to a fat woman, claimed that he would be all right because he could eat her. She laughed and clipped him round the ear. I have always been slim and now I was very thin. Everyone agreed that I was skin and bone and not worth eating. But despite their attempts to remain cheerful, there was an underlying atmosphere of anxiety and foreboding.

No one said anything, but their consciences seemed eased when Sheikh Fadlallah, the Shiites' religious leader and mentor of Hezbollah, said publicly that if one was starving, the eating of cats, dogs and, if necessary, human flesh, was not forbidden.

On 3 February, I wrote in my diary: 'The people are frightened and hungry and we can see it in their faces. I am still eating, but very little.' A few days later I noted: 'Very hungry and beginning to starve.'

We were trying to preserve what little food there was left in the hospital to feed the wounded and the staff. Families now completely without food had been gathering outside the hospital kitchen in increasing numbers at mealtimes, hoping for left-overs. There weren't any left-overs and the scenes became ever more frantic. One day, a man crazed by hunger shot a round of bullets into the kitchen ceiling.

I walked to my room one afternoon past 29 or so distraught people, mostly women and children, and including Ziad the urchin and his brothers and sisters, who were begging with bowls in their hands, pushing and shoving at the serving hatch, shouting at the kitchen women who were protesting that there was no spare food. I was so upset I burst into tears in my room.

'It's terrible,' I said to Souad, the nurse who was with me, 'that they should be reduced to this.'

'Please don't cry,' said Souad. 'This is our life.'

But what had they done to deserve it, I thought, exiled from their own country, unwanted, kicked around by host nations? The misery that I was experiencing for the first time was the daily lot of these people. They had endured it over and over again in the last 40 years. And it was not of their making. It was grossly unjust.

Although in the hospital we were still eating, albeit only about 400 calories a day, we were losing weight at an alarming rate. I lost 10 per cent of my body weight in two weeks and went right down to 43 kilograms. I watched the weight drop off Hannes and Dr Nader, both slim to begin with. One morning Hannes got up, keeled over dizzy and sick, and had to go back to bed. Dr Nader fainted during an operation. Their cheeks became hollow, their eyes sunk into their grey sockets and their bones became more prominent. Everyone's movements became slow and lethargic. The morning ward rounds seemed interminable and I had to keep sitting down. I could no longer hold my shoulders up straight. To stand up I had to push myself up with a hand on my knee. I knew I was slowly starving and, when someone offered me a spoonful of cooked dog, I accepted.

Even tea was running out. Nooha was drying out the used tea-leaves and reboiling them until the resulting liquid had almost no colour.

That week, two women suffering from malnutrition gave birth to babies prematurely. Both babies, underweight and sickly, died.

Four Palestinian men loaded up a truck with food in Mar Elias and made a mad dash for Bourj al Barajneh, shooting from the back. It was suicidal. As the truck raced from the airport road across the 60 metres of no man's land towards the camp, the Amal militia hit it with a rocket-propelled grenade, killing all four men and immobilising the truck. At night they attached a rope to it and winched it out of reach.

A few women and children simply walked out of the camp, no longer caring about the risk of being shot. Most were incarcerated in an empty school-building nearby but few followed their example, mindful of the fate of Hassan Halawani, one of the long-standing paraplegics. The timid male nurse looking after him could no longer bear to see him wasting away, so he put him in his wheelchair and pushed Hassan out of the camp to the airport road. They were caught by Amal militiamen who threw Hassan out of his chair and jumped on him. Later he was dumped outside Akka Hospital, frightened but little the worse for wear. They took the nurse away, and we heard nothing of him until two weeks later when he was released, badly beaten up and tortured, but alive.

We wrote another declaration, a desperate plea for help:

WE DECLARE THAT THE SITUATION IN THE BOURJ AL BARAJNEH CAMP HAS BECOME INTOLERABLE. THE CAMP HAS BEEN UNDER SIEGE FOR MORE THAN 14 WEEKS. TWO WEEKS AGO WE SENT OUT A DECLARATION THAT THERE SOON WOULD BE NO MORE FOOD IN THE CAMP AND THAT THE SITUATION WAS CRITICAL. WE ARE STILL UNDER SIEGE AND NOW THE PEOPLE ARE BEGINNING TO STARVE.

WE HAVE SEEN CHILDREN HUNTING IN GARBAGE HEAPS FOR SCRAPS OF FOOD. TODAY ONE WOMAN WAS SHOT WHILE TRYING TO COLLECT GRASS ON THE OUTSKIRTS OF THE CAMP TO BE ABLE TO FEED HER SEVEN CHILDREN WHO NO LONGER HAVE ANY FOOD AT ALL. SOME WOMEN AND CHILDREN ARE TAKING THE RISK OF LEAVING THE CAMP AND MANY SMALL CHILDREN HAVE BEEN TAKEN PRISONER. SOME OF THOSE WHO HAVE NO FOOD NOW EAT DOGS AND WILDCATS TO SURVIVE. WE APPEAL TO ALL PARTIES IN THIS WAR TO STOP FIGHTING, AND WE APPEAL TO THE UNITED NATIONS TO TAKE STEPS TO ACHIEVE A CEASE-FIRE IMMEDIATELY, SO THE INTERNATIONAL RELIEF ORGANISATIONS CAN GET IN WITH FOOD AND MEDICINES TO STOP THIS MASSACRE.

The next day we heard it quoted on the BBC World Service. I was mentioned by name. 'At last,' I thought. 'Surely something must happen.'

The psychological demoralisation of the hunger was somehow worse than the physical effects. In the second week of February, our morale went up and down wildly. Our hopes would rise when the efforts of UNRWA and the Iranians seemed to be succeeding, and ceasefires were announced to allow supplies to come in, only to plummet again when all we got were bombs.

These were very dangerous times. Every time there was a rumour that trucks were coming, people would eagerly come out of their shelters, then scatter as the shelling began. On 11 February, women and children, three generations from one family, were hit. One child, whom I had already operated on one month before, was killed and five were injured.

By now the world knew what was happening. We heard on the BBC that Arab governments and the EEC had pledged millions of pounds worth of aid and relief. The problem was how to get it into the camps. Nabih Berri was demanding that the Palestinians make further concessions east of Saida. The King of Morocco offered to drop in supplies from the air. This was not very realistic, but it showed that international political pressure was obviously building on Berri.

Lebanese internal political pressure was also evident. The Druze leader, Walid Jumblatt, was becoming discontented with his Amal allies, especially since 19 January when Amal militiamen ambushed one of his right-hand men and Mustafa Saad, the leader of the Saida Nasserites, and tried to kill them both in the neighbourhood of Ouzai, near the airport. On the evening of 8 February, George Hawi, leader of the Lebanese Communist Party, announced: 'We will not allow another Tel al Zatar massacre.'

At last people were beginning to speak up.

Chapter 14

The morning ward round of Friday the thirteenth of February was very depressing. An eleven-year-old boy and a six-year-old girl, who had been wounded two days previously, were dying from their infected wounds. We were helpless to prevent the infection because we had run out of antibiotics. We just had to stand by and watch these children die. I had had no breakfast and I already felt very weary.

We heard news of another ceasefire announcement with the promise of relief trucks, but we no longer believed such announcements.

The bombing began at 10 a.m. I went to the emergency room and watched with horror the first of the wounded being brought in. It was a teenage boy, covered in dust and rubble. Both his legs had been blown off. But before we had a chance to start working on him, more wounded were rushed in. Soon the scale of the catastrophe became apparent as more and more came in until there were seven men and boys, all with both legs amputated, and seven others, some of them with serious injuries. The emergency room looked like an abattoir.

A bomb had landed in the midst of a group of people sitting around drinking tea. I recognised Imad, a friend of Ben's, amongst the amputees. 'Help me,' he moaned in English. 'Please help me.' Two of those who had lost their legs died almost immediately. Panic gripped the onlookers and extended throughout the camp as the news spread. In the screaming mayhem which followed, we tried desperately to save the rest. Six needed major operations, the five amputees and one other. Dr Mounir shouted at me above the din, 'We have to try to do two at a time.'

Nooha took an ordinary trolley on wheels into the theatre to use as an operating table. We pushed past the crowds of people gathering outside the laboratory to give blood and told the porters to bring in the first two patients immediately. One was Imad. Adnan, the anaesthetic-technician, put them to sleep one after the other; the other staff, including Hannes, took turns to ventilate them by squeezing the bag while Adnan went between the two administering a bit of this and a bit of that to keep them asleep.

The amputees required formal amputations and four of us, Dr Rede, Dr Mounir, Dr Samer and myself, worked together two to a patient, bumping into each other in the cramped space of the tiny operating-theatre. We only had one bone saw and had to pass it from hand to hand. We worked quickly and finished the first two inside an hour, but it was exhausting work and I pleaded for someone to go out and ask in the camp for some tea. 'I don't think we can do all this without a cup of tea,' I gasped.

The bombing was still going on. People were running to the hospital to give blood. Others were bringing any old medicines, scraps of gauze, cotton wool, antiseptic, anything they had in their first-aid kits at home.

As we finished operating on the first two casualties, a bomb landed on the path to the hospital. Two more people were killed and another four wounded. We ran to the emergency room in our blood-drenched gowns. Someone was trying to pass a tube into a man I knew on the floor but I could see at once that he was already dead. 'Leave him!' I shouted. 'Take care of another one!'

At that moment, with almost no fuel and hardly any medicines, gauze or bandages, the problems seemed insurmountable, but we had no alternative other than to carry on. We took the next two amputees. While we were operating, someone rushed in with the news that trucks were entering the camp, escorted by the Iranians. But even with the escort they were fired on.

A Hezbollah driver was shot in the head and brought to the emergency room. He was resuscitated by Dr Aissam and Dr Nader and given blood. After negotiations, the Iranians were permitted to take him out. I never saw him. He was gone by the time we finished operating. The trucks were turned away.

Someone had brought tea, which kept us going. At 11 p.m. we finished operating and I ate my meal for that day – a tin of corned beef which I ate from the tin with a spoon.

The day was a bad dream, 6 dead, 18 wounded, 5 of them bilateral amputees including a father and his two sons.

All morning, a niggling fear had stabbed at the back of my mind. I knew that Ben often went to drink tea with his friend Imad in the morning. I knew also that two corpses had been taken straight to the morgue. I had not seen Ben all day and no one had mentioned him. The irrational thought that Ben was dead and in the fridge and no one had dared to tell me had grown in my mind, but I decided not to ask. If it were true, I could do nothing to change it and I would possibly not have been able to do all the work.

At the end of the day, Ben walked into the hospital, smiling, unaware of the irrational fear that had gripped my mind. 'Oh, Ben,' I said quietly, and hugged him.

The evening was quiet. The bombing had stopped. I was lying on my bed, exhausted, when a young man came to tell me that I was wanted on the walkie-talkie. Come quickly, he said, it was very important. The batteries in the hospital walkie-talkie were flat and I had to go out to an office of one of the political groups. Ben came with me. 'Hello,' I said. It was Jim Muir of the BBC. I knew his voice having heard it so often on the World Service. I told him of the day's events. Then, to my enormous surprise, I spoke to Dr Swee Chai Ang, the Malaysian doctor I had met at MAP. Then I heard the voices of my mother and father! I was completely astonished. A radio link to the BBC

176

in London via Cyprus had been set up and although the line was so bad I could only hear one word in ten, I was able to shout that I was all right, and that I was looking forward to eating my mother's stew and dumplings.

Jim Muir asked me how long it would be before people would be starving to death. I told him about the death of the two premature babies and that although it takes a long time to starve to death, without relief we would be seeing big problems within a week. He then asked me if I thought the appeals we had sent out had put me in personal danger and if we foreigners wanted to be 'rescued' from the camp.

The thought had not crossed my mind but, now it had been put to us, the idea of abandoning our patients and our colleagues and friends was so preposterous, I said, 'No, I'm not coming out until it's finished,' and Ben agreed.

As we walked back to the hospital in the moonlight, I said to Ben, 'We may die here, you know.' 'I know,' he said. After the events of the day, I was almost convinced that there would never be a ceasefire and that we would die in Bourj al Barajneh along with everyone else. In the hospital we sat in my room for a few minutes in the dark. We had nothing to eat, nothing to drink, and nothing to smoke.

'I don't regret coming here despite everything,' said Ben.

'No, neither do I,' I replied. 'I only regret that my family and friends will suffer. They did not choose this. I did.' My parents had instilled in me a strong sense of justice. What was happening here was unjust. I hoped they would understand that we could not leave now.

'I would like to write a letter home,' said Ben, 'explaining everything.'

'Yes. I've thought about that,' I said.

Then, through the open window, I heard the sound of a car engine. It can't be, I thought. Then I heard it again.

'I can hear a car!' I exclaimed, rushing over to the window to listen. 'It's in the camp, I'm sure it is. Come on.'

We stumbled downstairs in the dark and across the foyer

towards the front entrance. Blind in the darkness, I dashed straight into the wall in my excitement. I peered out of the doorway, not daring to go right outside. The beam of car headlights was coming towards the hospital. Ten yards away two cars stopped and four men got out. One was dressed in a smart jacket and had two cameras round his neck. He stopped about a yard away from me and peered at me in the moonlight.

'You're foreign,' he said, surprised. 'Which country are you from?'

'Who are you?' I asked, wondering how on earth they had got in and why it was so quiet.

'I'm a journalist with *Newsweek* magazine,' he said.

By this time Dr Rede had appeared with a few others and the man went away with Dr Rede.

The two cars were full of flour and milk-powder. They were driven by members of Hezbollah, who had apparently bribed the militiaman on guard to let them into the camp. This was an act of great courage, considering that their driver had been shot and killed earlier that day. They did not stay long. After 20 minutes the cars were unloaded and the Hezbollah men and the journalist, a Lebanese, had driven off into the night.

'I think this was the most bizarre and terrible day of my whole life,' I wrote in my diary.

Chapter 15

That Friday the thirteenth was the worst day. Those that followed were quieter. One of the amputees, the father, died from his associated injuries, but the others were doing well physically. The psychological disturbances caused by the loss of their legs were profound. As so often, it was the youngest boy who adapted most quickly. Soon he was doing exercises to strengthen his arms, instructed by Hannes.

But the older three went through phases of anger, frustration and depression. They were difficult with us and worse with their families, ordering them around and shouting at them. One wanted to be knocked out with Pethidine all the time and another managed somehow to get hold of some tranquillisers. The oldest, a man of about 35, kept recounting with bravado his former daring feats in battle. Changing his dressings was an ordeal for all. He would recite poetry at the top of his voice to try to take his mind off the pain. Some of the poetry was in English and I recognised a passage from 'The Rime of the Ancient Mariner'. But often he would just roar and bellow uncontrollably, occasionally gripping my arm until it hurt. Two weeks after he was injured, his wife gave birth to their fifth child. She remained calm and strong, even though I think she was alarmed at times by her husband's wild ramblings.

Changes of dressings were a problem. There was a severe shortage of bandages, and for sticking plaster we were using bright red-and-green insulating tape. Ben and Susie often did not have any gauze for their dressing changes and had to turn patients away. With the lack of clean dressing material and the effects of malnutrition many of the wounds became dirty.

Two days after that terrible Friday, on Sunday 15 February, I became very worried about one of my patients. A fourteen-year-old boy called Ali, he was one of those wounded by shrapnel on the path to the hospital. I had checked him over with Dr Dergham and as his wounds were not too serious I had left Dr Dergham to put in the chest tube and clean up his leg wounds, which were flesh wounds only. We had long since run out of intravenous penicillin but gave each of the amputees a single high dose of the last intramuscular penicillin. Ali, not so seriously wounded, had been given ampicillin only. Despite being elevated on pillows, Ali's wounded leg began to swell alarmingly and after two days the foot had a bluish hue. I took him to the operating-theatre and made two long incisions in his leg to relieve the increasing pressure, scooped out a collection of blood in the thigh and stopped a bleeding vessel. But it didn't help and the next day, when we took off his dressing under general anaesthetic, my worry increased. It was almost certainly gas gangrene developing. 'If we had had enough penicillin for Ali,' I thought, 'this would not be happening.' I told his family that his life was in danger and that if he was no better tomorrow we would have to amputate his leg. 'I'm afraid the chances of his keeping his leg are no better than one per cent,' I said sadly.

The next morning Ali was gone. His family had collected him from the hospital and taken him out of the camp at 6 a.m. We heard news that Amal had caught him and beaten him but not killed him. He had been admitted to a hospital in Beirut where the family had been told there was a 60 per cent chance of saving the leg; on hearing this they were disparaging about our advice. I hoped for the boy's sake that they were right.

Five days later his corpse was brought back into the camp. Dr Rede examined the body and told me that they had done a high amputation the day before, but too late. It was too much for Dr Dergham. His confidence was shattered and he disappeared from the hospital for several days. I blamed myself. If only I had amputated the leg when I had first suspected the gas gangrene, the boy would still have been alive. But the worst burden of guilt was borne by his family. I felt desperately sorry for them. From the whole terrible affair there was one tiny compensation. The bilateral amputees became a bit less bitter and angry. They knew that they at least were still alive.

When Dr Dergham reappeared in the hospital a few days later, I took him aside and told him that he must not feel responsible for Ali's death. 'I am the one who takes the responsibility,' I said. 'I am very proud of the work you have done in this war, as is everyone else, and you must be proud of it too.' He looked relieved and thanked me, then walked away to get on with his work.

The bread and milk brought by Hezbollah were luxurious. I dipped pieces of bread into hot sweet milk and savoured every mouthful. But distributed amongst the population of the camp it was enough for three days at most. 'We are all still losing weight,' I noted in my diary, 'despite the bread and milk. But not so terribly hungry as before.'

I spoke with more journalists on the walkie-talkie, including David Hirst of the *Guardian*, telling them about the situation in the camp and the arrival of the milk and flour. They told me that in the city there were fierce clashes between Amal militiamen and other groups of PSP and the Communist Party. The Sunni Murabitoun and Sunni Nasserites joined in until a battle was raging throughout West Beirut. On the night of 15 February, Susie and Ben heard the sound of tanks moving outside the camp and we assumed that they were moving away to support their troops in the city.

Then on the 16th it was announced that the women

181

would be allowed out from Rashidiye for five hours a day to get food. The following day a similar announcement was made for Bourj al Barajneh.

At last, after nearly four months, it seemed that the political pressures had paid off and that the end of the siege was in sight.

On 18 February, the first few women ventured out of Bourj al Barajneh to get fresh food. Only one entrance on the east side of the camp was opened and the women had to walk across 50 metres of open ground to an Amal checkpoint. There they were escorted to a local supermarket where they were forced to pay exorbitant prices, two or three times the normal, then taken back to the camp. They were body-searched by a woman in a scarf, some of their goods were confiscated, money and jewellery were stolen.

But that was not all. Four women were shot and more were shot at. There were similar scenes the following day. One woman was shot only a few yards away from the camp. Four men ran out to pick her up but they too were shot, one of them fatally. Subsequently only women went out to collect the wounded.

We were incredulous at first. The bitterness and anger of Amal seemed to know no bounds. But the courage of the women was incredible. They kept on going out in spite of the danger. Some of them managed to bring in fresh food.

Adham came to collect me for a meal of fried eggs, bread and spicy meatballs. The emotional relief at seeing food was almost too great to control and, as I saw the eggs cracked into the pan, my eyes filled with tears.

Over the next week our incredulity turned to anger and resentment. Every day the women went out they were harassed or shot at. A fourteen-year-old girl was brought dead to the hospital shot through the head. Her mouth was full of food.

Meanwhile, the battles in West Beirut increased in ferocity and 150 people were killed in a matter of days.

Amal were being slowly driven back out of the city and the infamous Murr Tower, where it was thought they held hundreds of prisoners, was surrounded.

Then, on the night of 21 February, almost without warning, Syrian troops, between 6,000 and 10,000 men with tanks and armoured cars, rolled into West Beirut to quell the fighting. They drove back the forces surrounding the Murr Tower and, when they entered it several days later, it was empty. As the Syrians put their security plan into operation, the militias disappeared off the streets, the Druze into their heartland of the Chouf Mountains and the Amal into the southern suburbs. In revenge for the part played by the Communist Party in the fighting, 10 doctors and dentists working for the Secours Populaire Lebanaise were killed by Shiites in the south of Lebanon.

On 25 February our morale was raised again when two UNRWA trucks full of food were allowed into the camp. To get permission, UNRWA had had to give two truckloads of food to the Amal militia for the Shiite population.

At first, people ventured out only cautiously, half expecting shelling. But none came and eventually I could not contain my curiosity. The arrival of the trucks was a major event, not just because they brought food and some medicines, but because it was a chance to meet people from the outside world. We had felt so cut off for so long. I walked a few yards out from the front of the hospital, past the vast garbage mountain, when I was confronted by a photographer. Before I could say anything he had taken my picture.

The UNRWA official in charge of the unloading of the trucks, a woman sent from their headquarters in Vienna, looked a bit shocked by conditions in the camp. She enquired politely how I was.

'Much better seeing you,' I told her.

She asked me one or two more questions about what we needed, then she paused, reached into her pocket and said, 'And here's my card.'

I looked at it in astonishment. A beautiful white visitor's card, it seemed to come from another world.

'Thank you,' I said, and put it in my pocket.

Slowly, the Syrians restored some order in West Beirut, but not without some bloodshed. In clearing out the Hezbollah barracks in Basta on 24 February, 23 Hezbollah were killed. Furious, they retired into the southern suburbs accusing the Syrians of having perpetrated a 'massacre'.

The Syrians kept saying that soon they would be advancing into the southern suburbs. We expected them any day. One quiet evening I went down to the clinic for a break and to get warm. It was still wet and cold, near freezing at times, and without electricity the hospital was like an ice-box.

Ben had been given a small wood-burning fire, a tin box with a grate, on legs. Having burned all the spare wood we, like many of the camp's inhabitants, were now burning the furniture. A broken chair had gone and Ben chopped up a bookcase.

I was sitting on the floor, warming myself by the fire, when suddenly I heard the sound of bombs flying over us and exploding in the camp. We could hear the 'tok' as they were launched in salvoes of three or four a few seconds apart. I knew that I must get to the hospital. I waited until the third salvo went over and then sprinted before the next was launched.

It was terrifying. Never had it seemed so far or such a steep climb to the hospital, but I dared not stop running. I arrived breathless and sweating, with an ache in my chest and legs. When I dashed into the emergency room there were no wounded and the others laughed at me. 'Running under the bombs', they called it. I thought of the stretcher-bearers who had to do it regularly and – carrying the dead and wounded – could not run so fast. It was a minor miracle that none had yet been seriously wounded.

The weeks went by and still there was no sign of the

Syrians. Nabih Berri declared that the siege of Bourj al Barajneh was lifted, but as each day passed we became more bitter as the women allowed out to get food continued to be intimidated, abused, beaten, robbed, shot at and killed. The women were still only allowed to use the one exit and they called it 'Death Passage'. Gathering at the exit every morning at about 5.30 a.m., they waited for permission to go out. Most days it was granted and they were allowed out to the shops. But when they returned, their goods were all checked. Certain items were forbidden: candles, batteries, sometimes coffee. Cigarettes were rationed, any medicines or gauze and fuel of any kind were confiscated.

If fuel was discovered secreted in bottles of shampoo or drinks it was poured all over the shopping, which was set on fire. Many items and money were stolen. Any woman who protested was beaten, abused or shot at.

Amal practised systematic intimidation. They would stand the woman against a wall as if for a firing squad, then shoot around their feet, making them crawl on the ground. One girl told me an Amal militiaman had said to her. 'Where do you want to be shot? In the legs, the chest or the head?' and to another, 'They are nice shoes. Take them off so I can shoot you in the foot.'

When Hassan's mother went out, she was chased, her shopping rifled and then she was shot at as she tried to run into the camp carrying a heavy sack on her head and two bags in her hands. She was still crying with anger and fear when I saw her a few hours later.

By 10 March, 8 women had been killed and about 25 wounded as they passed through Death Passage. And they still kept running the gauntlet every few days because each time they could only carry enough food for several days and the threat of hunger was still present.

On 12 March we made another declaration, describing how the women were being shot and the appalling conditions in Bourj al Bourajneh. It ended: 'How long will this

185

misery continue for the people of this camp? We appeal to the UN to intervene urgently to put an end to this suffering.'

I was appalled by the brutality of Amal. A young man called Abu Bashar knew some of the Amal militiamen of old. They called out to him to come out across the wasteland to drink tea with them. At first he was suspicious and would not go. But after repeated reassurances – 'On the Koran we will not harm you' – he ventured out, sat down and drank tea with them. He gave them some money to buy bread and powdered milk for his young baby. When he was walking back to the Palestinian front-line after his third such visit, the Amal militiamen opened fire without warning. Abu Bashar was shot dead in his tracks.

Permission was shouted to four women to pick him up on a stretcher. As they started back to the camp with his body, they too were shot. One had a broken thigh. It took her half an hour to crawl back into the safety of the camp. She was carried, filthy and in shock, into the emergency room, where we were waiting. As well as her broken thigh, she had multiple cuts on her hands and legs.

They had dropped the stretcher when the shooting started, Abu Bashar lay outside for 10 days until, under a barrage of covering fire from the camp, two Palestinians ran out and brought back his body. He was buried at once.

The siege went on, 'We are all dying very slowly,' said Dr Mounir.

We were not alone. The military assault was now concentrated on Chatila and the information coming out of the camp was that they too were facing starvation.

On two consecutive days, 10 and 11 March, we heard that the International Red Cross were coming into Bourj al Barajneh. We prepared detailed reports on all the patients in the hospital and those at home who needed specialist follow-up. But the Red Cross didn't come. We learned on the radio that they had tried to get into Chatila with a Syrian escort, but were attacked and had withdrawn. We felt more isolated than ever.

On 13 March, Adham's mother got safely out of the camp and went straight to the Syrian headquarters in the Beau Rivage Hotel. She told the head of Syrian Military Intelligence about the women being shot and demanded that he intervene. He told her that maybe after 10 days he might do something.

The freezing cold lasted well into mid-March, unusual for the Lebanon. I saw another child with frost-bite on her toes. People had no fuel, much of the wood in the camp had already been burned, and they could not heat what remained of their houses.

In the hospital it was impossible to get warm. The shelling was now sporadic and infrequent and most of the daily work was treating the women and others who had been sniped. After dark the snipers could not see to do their deadly work, so evenings were usually quiet. I would go down to the clinic to warm myself by the wood fire. Ben and Susie were burning the second bookcase. If we closed the doors it was warm but very smoky; we got covered in soot and our clothes smelled of smoke. If we opened the doors, the chill wind howled through.

The inescapable damp and cold in the hospital depressed and demoralised me and my evenings with Ben and Susie were a great comfort. We had been given rations of milk and flour from the supplies delivered by UNRWA and we drank hot milk or, when a friend brought some eggs, made pancakes.

The distribution of flour — one kilogram per head of population — established the real population of Bourj al Barajneh as 9,000. I was surprised. Before 1982 it was 30,000, so that meant 20,000 or more had left.

In the clinic I was also able to take a bath of sorts. I heated up water in an enormous saucepan, then stood in a large bowl and poured the warm water over myself. It was such luxury it was worth all the effort of getting the water and heating it over the wood fire. I had similar baths in the hospital when the women heated up the water, but the fires there were usually heating water for washing the linen and I usually only managed a bath once every 10 days. My room was still an icy lake, which always managed to claim at least one article of clean clothing whenever I took a bath.

It was good to be with Susie. I had seen little of her in the past months. I admired her. She had worked hard and never complained, even when she was wounded in the arm, though she later admitted it had hurt like hell. But now I was concerned about her. She had a chronic cough which had not cleared up after six weeks, despite two courses of antibiotics. We were all run-down and undernourished and I began to worry that she had TB. When one day she developed a sudden pain in the right side of her chest I insisted that she be X-rayed, but the tests revealed nothing.

One evening, coughing as she laughed, she told me about one of the teenage fighters who had come to her asking for a piece of sticking plaster. Plaster for wounds was extremely scarce and she demanded to know what it was for.

'He came in,' she said, 'clutching something gingerly between his hands. I thought at first it was a wounded bird, but then he said, "The pin has come loose on my grenade and it's not stable." I screamed at him, "Get out of the clinic! Go outside! Out, out, before you blow us all to bits!" He tiptoed out again and somehow one of the older men stabilised the grenade.'

On 14 March at 10.30 in the morning we got a surprise. UNRWA managed to bring in two more food trucks, again by giving two to Amal. The trucks contained flour, sugar, milk and rice. They were not allowed to bring in medicines, but the food was very welcome as for two days the women had been forbidden to leave the camp.

This time I met two middle-aged men in suits from UNRWA in the administrators' office. Everybody wanted to talk to them and the tiny office was crowded. We told them about conditions in the camp and the state of the hospital – mouldy, filthy, wet, unstable in parts and now without many medicines, anaesthetics, fuel and basic stocks of bandages and gauze. They were shocked.

'How do you manage to bath?' one asked.

'We don't take a bath, we take a bucket,' I replied.

'And only every ten days,' said Dr Mounir.

'Don't tell them that,' I said. 'They won't come again.'

A photographer traipsed around the camp with me in the pouring rain, picking his way through the overflowing sewage and garbage in his smart Italian grey leather shoes. He took pictures of me, of the inhabitants and their children, of Ben and Susie in the clinic. Then we returned to the hospital.

I was walking towards the UNRWA food store next to the hospital with one of the UNRWA officials when little Ziad appeared. He tugged at my white coat and gazed up at me.

'What does he want?' asked the man.

'He's a beggar,' I replied. 'I used to give him money but I don't have any.'

The man reached into the pocket of his suit and pulled out some notes and coins. He thrust them into Ziad's up-stretched hands. It was so much money – more than Ziad had ever been given before – that some dropped on the ground. I laughed as he gathered up every last coin and ran off whooping with joy.

The visit from UNRWA raised our spirits temporarily. But the euphoria was short-lived. A girl was brought in dead, shot through the heart. I recognised her at once and let out a cry of anguish. It was Suzanne, one of my first patients in Bourj al Barajneh, the girl I had operated on at the beginning of my stay in the Lebanon and who had proudly shown me the new shoes she could now wear.

Chapter 16

Haifa Hospital had become a symbol of resistance in the camp and we were determined not to stop working, but everyone knew we were still desperately short of fuel, medicines and gauze. Some women tried to bring in medical supplies under their dresses and in their underwear, but if they were discovered they risked a beating and the vital supplies were confiscated.

The wife of Salah, the head nurse, was questioned one morning about the hospital by a group of Amal militiamen. 'Yes, it is still working very well,' she told them defiantly.

They did not seem at all happy at the news. 'And who is working in there?' they demanded to know.

Salah's wife mentioned a few names and a 'foreign doctor'.

They scowled. 'Yes, we know about her,' they said angrily. 'We are going to cut her into pieces.'

For a few days, no one told me of this, but when I was talking to Dr Rede one morning, I said, 'If I ever get out of here I want to go to Saida for a holiday.' He replied, 'I don't think that will be possible,' and told me what had been said.

I have to confess that I was frightened. I had known that speaking out exposed us as named individuals, but I was not prepared to remain silent and even this direct threat changed nothing. 'The truth cannot be cut to pieces,' I thought. 'I will not be silenced.'

That night I thought again about writing a letter to my family, to be opened 'in the event of my death'. 'I'll do it tomorrow,' I wrote in my diary, but in the event I didn't.

A few days after learning of the threats against my life, a

stranger appeared in the hospital during our morning ward round. It was the very same journalist who had come in with the Hezbollah and the Iranians. He arrived alone, totally unannounced, and seemed nervous and uneasy. He wanted photos of the doctors, but especially he wanted to take a photograph of me. Indeed he did not seem very interested in anything else. After he had taken a couple of pictures he asked permission to fix up his flash. I became more suspicious. 'Why a photo of me,' I thought, 'and how did he get into the camp on his own? All the entrances are controlled by Amal.' In a moment of paranoia I thought, 'He has been sent by them to take my picture so they will know what I look like when they come to kill me.'

I was not the only one who was suspicious about him. 'Do you trust him?' I whispered to Dr Rede.

'No, not entirely,' he replied.

Salah also advised, 'Don't let him take your photo. We don't know who he is.'

I became more and more uneasy and eventually I told him, 'If you take my photo after I have asked you not to, I will tell them to take your film away.'

After that he left, but he returned, undaunted, with a video camera. This time he had gone first to the camp committee, one of whom knew him and verified his credentials as a bona fide journalist. I was very apologetic; he had braved the dangers of getting into the camp and paid a lot of money to a Lebanese soldier to help him – and I had refused to co-operate. So this time Susie and I consented to a lengthy videotaped interview, which he said was for ITN in England.

A few days later, at dusk, one of the hospital porters came running to find me. He shouted in garbled Arabic, 'There is a man here. Come, come, foreign, foreign, English, English!' I followed him to the administrator's office and stared with disbelief at Brent Sadler, an ITV journalist I recognised from having seen him on the television in England. He was sitting with the same Lebanese journalist who had made the video. I was terribly excited. I had so much to tell him, and I plied him with questions about what was happening outside and at home in England. I took him to meet Hannes, then down to the clinic to see Ben and Susie. We talked into the night.

'You seem so cheerful,' he commented at one point.

'We are so happy to see you,' we told him.

That same day four girls between the ages of 7 and 13 had come to see Dr Rede in the hospital. 'We think we can get out and back into the camp over the sand-hills,' said the eldest. 'We will go to Mar Elias and collect medicines.' They left at once, reached Mar Elias safely and stayed there overnight.

The following morning they reappeared, triumphant. They had succeeded in sneaking in from the airport road over the sand-hills with four carrier-bags full of medicines, bandages and gauze.

Brent Sadler asked them to carry the bags to the front of the hospital so they could be filmed. 'What will happen if they are caught?' he asked me.

'Until now they have not been seen,' I told him, 'and as they are only children I don't think they would be harmed.'

His question was prophetic. The girls went out again that same night and, returning the following morning, were spotted by Brent Sadler as he was filming in the cemetery. He turned his camera on the girls as they crossed the distant sand-hills. At that moment they were seen and a fusillade of bullets raised puffs of sand around them. They dived to the ground, then pelted down into the cemetery, into the arms of the waiting men. They were frightened but miraculously unharmed.

Brent Sadler and the Lebanese journalist stayed for two days, making a film about Bourj al Barajneh. They interviewed both Susie and me. On the morning of the day they were due to leave, someone brought a video machine and a television to the hospital so that we could watch the videotapes while the generator was on for an operation. People crowded into the room next to the operating-theatre and the four girls were given seats at the front. When they saw themselves on television they jumped to their feet in excitement.

Brent brought Susie, Ben and I a cassette tape and a small recorder so that we could tape messages for our families. We tried hard to sound cheerful, sending our love and saying that we were healthy and happy.

As darkness fell, Brent and the Lebanese journalist crept out of the camp again.

The daily shooting of the women, if and when they were allowed out, continued, so the women staged a demonstration. They wanted permission to go out from the airport road exit, which was safer as it was guarded by soldiers of the official Lebanese Army. Three hundred or so women gathered near the airport road but were sent back to the camp. The next day, even more collected in the same place, but this time, after refusing an order from Amal to use the other exit, they were scattered by a sudden heavy bombardment of the camp. They ran for cover in all directions and some were wounded.

Dr Dergham had never quite returned to normal after his crisis over Ali, the boy who developed gas gangrene. Morose and gloomy, he moved out of the doctors' room down to a small deserted area in the basement. He went to bed in the early evening, then got up and sat with the night nurses before doing his allocated work at six or seven in the morning. This was eccentric enough, but one day the nurses told me that he had woken a patient at 5 a.m. in order to change his dressing.

I spoke with Sol-Britt and Øyvind on the walkie-talkie, and they told me they were trying to bring in relief medical staff, both foreign and Palestinian. But when they visited the office of Nabih Berri he told them that there was no need for a medical team in Bourj al Barajneh. He also informed them that 'supermarkets' were open in the camp. I was incensed. There were no supermarkets, and the only items left for sale in the shops were large numbers of electric light-bulbs as, without electricity, they were less than useless.

For two days we were miserable. Sporadic bombing began again and the news from Chatila was grim. They had an outbreak of typhoid – three cases at least. Without a clean water-supply, they were scooping rainwater out of bomb craters. Their food stocks were finished and they too were now facing starvation. Dr Rede was pessimistic. 'They may prolong this war to try to take Chatila,' he said. 'They are hitting them hard, which is why it has become quieter here.'

Then our spirits were raised again by the arrival of two more journalists, Marie Colvin and Tom Stoddart from the *Sunday Times*. It seemed that if one had the resources it was becoming quite easy to bribe one's way into the camp.

We took them on a tour of Bourj al Barajneh and looked after them as best we could. We gathered some food from friends near the clinic – reheated rice and tinned fish from the day before, and some tomatoes and cheese – but Tom, the photographer, could only eat a couple of mouthfuls. I think his lack of appetite can be ascribed partly to fear, partly to guilt at eating our food – Tom said he was 'well-padded' – and partly to the fact that to an outsider it must have seemed extremely unappetising. We had long ceased to care, eating everything put before us.

Marie, an attractive woman in her late twenties with a mass of curly brown hair, was an object of enormous interest for some of the young men, but eventually she and Susie extricated themselves from the throng of admirers and went to sleep with a family nearby. I took Tom up to the hospital.

Just as we were saying goodnight to Marie we saw a bright red flash and felt the shock-wave of a deafening explosion. We all jumped, Tom's cameras clanking round his neck. 'That was TNT,' said one of the young men casually.

In the hospital awaited a worse nightmare for Tom. A huge rat was scampering around the corridors. 'Not rats,' Tom moaned as I chased it down the stairs. 'They're the one thing I'm really frightened of.'

I left him to sleep in a cubicle next to Hannes, and went off to bed. I don't think he slept a wink, lying awake all night watching for rats under his bed.

The following day Marie and Tom were confronted with the true horror of life in Bourj al Barajneh. They saw a young woman shot through the head and abdomen just outside the camp. For half an hour she lay there as the bullets of the snipers kept people away. They made frantic efforts to haul her in with a rope. Eventually two girls dashed out and dragged her in.

In the hospital, Tom took photos as we tried vainly to resuscitate the injured woman. We did not have enough fuel for the necessary operation, so in the end a group of women carried her out to the airport road and to a hospital in the city.

Marie interviewed some of the patients in the hospital. The woman who had crawled in with the broken thigh spoke to her vehemently, gesturing with her arms. 'What's the matter with her?' asked Marie.

'She wants you to tell the world her story,' I translated. And a few days later Marie did just that.

When the time came for Tom and Marie to leave they looked a picture of misery as they sat waiting for the moment to cross the wasteland. 'I feel like Butch Cassidy and the Sundance Kid before they had to jump off that cliff,' said Tom.

One quiet evening after dark Adham took Ben and I to his

front-line position. 'Walk on this side,' he instructed, 'the other is exposed.' He switched off his torch and led us down into a small courtyard surrounded by white houses with overhanging balconies. In the centre of the courtyard a small tree rustled in the breeze. The scene was eerily beautiful in the moonlight.

Adham took my arm and pointed to a building across the wasteland. 'See that,' he whispered. 'Sometimes they shoot women from there.'

As we made our way back to the hospital Adham told us that his dream was to go to Cambridge University to read engineering. He had been studying at the Arab University, but did not think he could go back. 'As a Palestinian I would not be safe in West Beirut,' he said with a shrug. He had missed nearly six months' lectures and tutorials. I promised to find out what qualifications he would need for Cambridge, but in my heart I knew it would remain a dream. The fees alone were prohibitive.

Adham said something else that night – something I shall never forget. Describing how imprisoned he felt within the confines of the camp, he quoted Byron: 'I had no thought, no feeling, none – among the stones I stood a stone.'

At the beginning of April it at last began to get warm. The situation improved too. Fewer women than before were being shot at and many were allowed easier passage. Amal still engaged in petty harassment, though. They now insisted that the women buy the Amal magazine every Friday; one woman who refused was shot.

There were the usual rumours that the Syrians and the International Red Cross were on their way, but I had long ceased to believe them. 'I'll believe it when I see them,' I said.

But this time the rumours were true. On 7 April the Syrians deployed around Chatila. The next day they arrived at Bourj al Barajneh. The shooting stopped at once. For the first day in five and a half months, the hospital register showed the admission of no new wounded.

The Syrians were greeted with mixed feelings – relief at the end of the fighting, and resentment that they had waited six weeks before coming. During those six weeks 18 women had been killed and more than 50 wounded. Some people still felt that the Syrians bore the responsibility for the Camp Wars.

The next day the International Red Cross arrived with 12 cars. We had no critical patients now, but the hospital was so badly damaged, our stocks were all gone, and the staff were so exhausted, that we decided to send out as many patients as we could.

The scene was chaos. Hordes of journalists had come in with the Red Cross, including Julie Flint of the *Guardian*, who had interviewed me once after the first fighting. People were shouting, crowding round their relatives. Some patients who were almost fully recovered wanted to go out just to escape; others, who did need further treat-ment, refused to go, preferring to stay in Haifa than risk the open road. The woman, who had been shot in the legs while collecting grass to feed her family, had been in traction for nearly two months. As they came to carry her out she burst into tears and clasped me in her arms. I cried too.

As the convoy of cars departed, a crowd surged behind it to the border of the camp, some of them still hopeful of getting out. But the Syrian soldiers barred their way.

An hour or so later Øyvind arrived, bringing relief medical staff for the hospital – a British surgeon called Dr Alberto Gregori, Françoise, a French nurse, and a young Palestinian doctor.

After 163 days the siege was over, but Bourj al Barajneh still had its surprises. A friend of Ben's told us about an old woman who had lived in a building in the most dangerous part of the front line throughout the entire war. I couldn't believe it.

'Come,' he said. 'We can go and see her. It's quite safe now.'

Ben, Alberto and I followed him through the maze of alleyways to the north-east corner of the camp. There we crossed a narrow road to a five-storey building standing on its own. 'We had to dig a trench to get across here safely,' said Ben's friend.

The destruction of the buildings around the edge of the camp was unbelievable. Many of the houses I had known had been completely levelled, all of them were severely damaged. The building next to the one we were entering had completely collapsed, its five floors folding in on themselves like a fallen house of cards.

The young man led us up to the second floor of the apartment block next door. There, in a room, barricaded on all sides by mattresses, wardrobes and chairs so that there was only a tiny space in the middle, sat an enormously fat old woman wearing a scarf and a long nightdress.

'She is Lebanese,' explained the young man. 'She is so fat she cannot walk, and so she could not leave. She used to live on the fourth floor, but one night we heard her screaming and found that the floor above her was on fire.' It was Imad, Ben's friend who had later lost both legs, who had run into the building and helped her crawl down the stairs to her present room. Then he put out the fire.

'We bring her food and water every day and empty her bedpan,' said the young man.

'Yes,' said the woman, 'these boys have been very good. They looked after me all the time.'

With the lifting of the siege the first shop opened up in the camp. The woman who ran it had managed to bring in a few sackloads of goods. The news spread rapidly and, by the time I arrived, hoping to buy some eggs, there were 50 people crowded around the door, shouting and shoving. I was just deciding whether or not to join the fray when I was rescued by Adham. 'Come through here,' he beckoned, and led me into the parlour.

The shopkeeper was sitting on the floor holding a sort of auction. She was selling various items of food and cigarettes, and had a large wad of money stuffed inside her blouse. I had treated her once when she was very ill, so – much to my embarrassment – she decided to serve me first. I ordered some cheese and she asked for a knife to cut some from the big block in front of her.

Omar, a big man who was always a bit wild and had become noticeably crazier during the fighting, leapt to his feet. 'I've got a knife!' he bellowed, flourishing a large flick-knife and making sweeping cuts in the air.

Someone calmed him down, cut the cheese, and I crept out just as Ben arrived to buy some tobacco. We walked back to the clinic laughing.

Chapter 17

As the relief medical staff began to take over the work in the hospital, the Palestinian doctors I had worked with throughout the siege were able to leave the camp for a holiday. I couldn't go out but was able to take some rest.

The day Alberto Gregori had arrived, two patients with acute appendicitis were brought into the hospital. He watched the first operation in which I assisted Dr Samer, and then performed the second, so he was able to meet the operating-theatre staff and become an integral part of the team immediately. Tall, dark-haired and heavily built, Alberto seemed easy-going and with a fine sense of humour, and I could see he was a good surgeon. The staff liked him and trusted him straightaway. I had started to think about leaving the camp and, now that Alberto was here and taking over the work, the idea of going was made a little easier.

I was accompanying Alberto on the morning ward rounds two days later when a nurse rushed up and said that Dr Swee Chai Ang was in the hospital. I ran to the nurses' station and there she was. She hugged me, saying that she was so relieved to see that we were alive and well. I had forgotten how small Swee was. Even I, at 5′ 3″, towered over her and although I knew she was older than me she looked so young, almost like a child. But I also knew that she was tough and determined, having made her career in orthopaedic surgery, which is not easy for anyone, let alone a woman of 4′ 10″.

Ben, Susie and Hannes came to see Swee that evening. She asked us how soon we could all leave. Our families had been desperately worried about us and it was time to go. We all looked at each other, finding it hard to believe that the moment had come at last. Then I said, 'We must stay at least another two days. We need to pack and there are so many people to say goodbye to.'

We should have asked for longer because those two days were not long enough to make all our farewell visits. We were feasted and fed in so many households we could scarcely walk and all day there was a constant stream of visitors to the clinic, which slowed down our packing. Hassan's mother cried and hugged us and wouldn't let go. I kept looking for Adham and when he didn't come I went down to his house. He wasn't there. His mother explained that he had sneaked out of the camp to friends in West Beirut to try to sort out his university studies. I asked her to say goodbye for us, and got another hug.

On the morning of our departure we gathered with our luggage in the hospital and made a last round of farewells. It felt somehow unreal that we were actually leaving after such a long and traumatic time which we had endured with these people. I was also anxious about the threats that had been made against us. I began to get impatient. I wanted to get it over with.

At last Swee arrived at about 11.30 a.m. and we walked towards the edge of the camp surrounded by a crowd of about 50 people. Hassan was carrying my bag. When we reached the perimeter, the Syrian soldiers would not allow the people to go any further. As we walked towards the airport road to the two waiting cars I looked back and saw all the people gathered at the edge of the camp. It nearly broke my heart. We could go home to safety and comfort, but they could not even venture out one metre from the camp.

At the junction of the airport road and the side-road leading to the camp, the scene was typically chaotic. Swee had arranged Syrian escorts for us and each of the two white Mercedes waiting for us contained a driver and a passenger, presumably the escort. But as there was another doctor leaving with us, and Swee was also taking two foreign volunteers into Chatila, there was not enough room for us all. At the same time a hearse carrying a coffin was coming into the camp and the Syrian soldiers at the checkpoint were busy prising off the lid to make sure it was indeed carrying a dead body for burial.

Eventually Susie, myself and the Palestinian doctor got into one car, Swee and the two new volunteers into the other and a Syrian soldier stopped a passing car on the airport road and ordered the driver to follow with Ben and Hannes.

We all arrived at Mar Elias camp and assembled in the PRCS clinic. At last I was able to thank in person the doctor in charge who had co-ordinated information and relayed our messages during the siege. He had lived and slept in his office next to the radio walkie-talkie for nearly six months.

Dr Rede followed us to Mar Elias. As the director he wanted to be the last to leave.

Then, to my joy and astonishment, Adham walked in. He had got news of our departure and come to say goodbye. We shook hands. It would not have been the done thing to embrace, but I knew I would miss him terribly.

We bade an emotional farewell to our colleagues, then taxis took us from Mar Elias to the British Consulate where we were picked up by the British ambassador in his bomb-proof Jaguar and two Range Rover escorts. He was very kind to us and took us across the Green Line into East Beirut and up to his residence in the hills just above the city. There we experienced a sort of reverse culture-shock as we spread our napkins on our laps and ate a delicious meal of soup, chicken and vegetables and pudding at a highly polished wooden table in a spacious, luxuriously carpeted dining-room, served from silver trays by waiters in white jackets with gold buttons. In the evening Mr Gray, the ambassador, took us down to the port of Jounieh and we boarded the ferry.

At 5.30 a.m. the next morning, dishevelled and disorientated, blinking in the early morning sunlight, we wandered down the gangplank on to the quayside of Larnaca in Cyprus. Waiting for us were half a dozen journalists, a bunch of television crews, and a man from the PRCS in Cyprus. That they were waiting for us at such a horribly early hour was the first real indication that we as individuals had become a big news story. They surged around us, bombarding us with questions. It was reassuring to see the familiar face of Brent Sadler who had come into the camp some weeks previously and carried out the precious video showing the state of affairs inside the camp.

Some of the journalists suggested that we should all go to a nearby hotel for a 'chat over breakfast'. Breakfast sounded a wonderful idea, so we agreed. When we got to the hotel I was handed a telephone and Susie another. I was linked up first with my mother in one television studio and then with my father in another. A journalist stood beside me as we talked. I pointed to my open mouth and was brought a cup of tea. But when it was all over and we left the journalists to it, neither Susie nor I had managed to get a mouthful of breakfast.

'We starve for months in the camp,' I said indignantly to Susie, 'and now they cheat us out of breakfast.' We both burst out laughing.

We were tired, dirty and confused and were unanimous in wanting at least a day's rest before the journey to England and what we now suspected would be a barrage of questions. Some friends booked us into a quiet hotel on the sea. We phoned our families to tell them when we would arrive home and they told us a little more about what to expect. It seemed that, for the moment at least, we were famous. It felt rather strange to us to be heralded as heroes, because we had all seen acts of courage and heroism beyond anything any of us had done.

In the evening in the hotel, the tension and stress finally

lifted and we became very giggly over a bottle of wine, switching the electric light on and off and turning the hot-water tap on repeatedly like children and laughing help-lessly. The next day we boarded the plane to London. Tele-vision crews accompanied us on the plane, and at Heathrow in the early morning we were met by a wall of press and photographers and, at last, our families. There were my mother, father and brother, and our colleagues from MAP, but we hardly had time to speak as we were swept along to a press conference.

At last, in the evening, Susie and her family, Ben and I were able to relax at my parents' home. But every now and then during the celebration I would see Susie or Ben staring into the middle distance, no longer listening, and I knew they were back in the camp, as I was, thinking of the people with whom we had lived during those severe and terrible months and whom we had left behind.

Epilogue

On 4 June 1987 I woke up early and anxious. At last the day had come. The two boys, Bilal and Samir, were arriving today. I hoped there would be no last-minute problems. 'Please, no more delays,' I thought. Until they were on the plane out of Beirut I could not be sure of anything. If fighting broke out, Beirut airport could close at a moment's notice. It had been extremely difficult and time-consuming to arrange their travel documents, especially for Bilal who, as a Palestinian, was not entitled to a passport and had to be given the usual '*laissez-passer*'. Samin was a Lebanese Shiite boy so to arrange a passport was easier. The whole process had taken more than six weeks despite the persistence and pleas of urgency to the passport office officials from Dr Swee Chai Ang who was in Beirut making the arrangements.

At lunchtime I got a message from Cyprus, where the plane touched down. They were on their way.

These two small boys, both victims of the terrible civil war in the Lebanon, were coming to England to be treated at the world-famous Stoke Mandeville Hospital. Bilal, aged seven, was an old friend; I remembered the day he had been brought into Haifa Hospital and I had discovered that he was paralysed from the waist down. Samir was eight and his spine too had been shattered by a bullet. A bullet was still lodged in his neck. For injuries like these, there was no better place than Stoke Mandeville.

By 5.30 p.m. I was waiting impatiently at Heathrow airport. At last I got a message that they had landed and were in the medical centre. I felt so sorry for them at that moment. They were tired and completely disorientated.

Bilal's mother who had come with them was bewildered and she burst into tears and hugged me when she saw me. Because both boys were paralysed, a team of a nurse and an ambulance driver who specialised in transporting patients with spinal injuries were there to look after them and take them to Stoke Mandeville. Bilal had been washed and changed but poor Samir was crying and protesting and would not take his clothes off. Even Swee, who had come with them and whom Samir trusted, could not persuade him. We decided not to upset him further and to set off for Stoke Mandeville. Outside the medical centre they were met by a wall of photographers, cameras clicking and flashing. I was worried that it might make them cry, but they kept their composure and were soon loaded into the ambulance and on their way out of the airport.

Samir soon fell asleep, but Bilal and his mother chattered away in Arabic to the nurse and me. I asked Bilal's mother about the situation in Bourj al Barajneh.

'It's better,' she answered. 'There is no fighting. But the men still do not go out for fear of kidnapping and beating or arrest. There is still no electricity or running water in most houses in the camp and no rebuilding is allowed. But people are happy that the fighting is stopped.'

As we approached the hospital I told her, 'You will meet Mr Nuseibeh the doctor and Jimmy Savile. Jimmy is a very very good man. He will pay for the treatment of Bilal and Samir.' I remembered how Jimmy Savile, one of Britain's best-known radio and television personalities, had heard me mention the boys in an interview and had appeared on breakfast television and offered to pay for them to go to Stoke Mandeville Hospital. An indefatigable supporter of the hospital, he had previously raised 10 million pounds for the spinal injuries unit there. His offer was extraordinarily generous, but on top of that he had also offered help and advice in private about arrangements and when would be the best time for the press to meet the boys at the hospital.

As we drove in through the gates of Stoke Mandeville Hospital, there was Jimmy, unmistakeable with his ash-blond hair and smoking a large cigar, standing on his own at the entrance in a hospital porter's coat. I giggled and waved.

When the boys were settled in their rooms, Jimmy came to see them and within two minutes had them both laughing. The misery of the day's long journey was forgotten. I tried to thank Jimmy but I could not find the right words to express my gratitude. Thanks to this man these two small boys had been given the chance to make the best of the rest of their lives.

As I left them to the care of the night nurses and tiptoed into the corridor, I thought about the thousands of people in the Lebanon, adults and children, Palestinians and Lebanese, disabled by the civil war, who had no such opportunity and I determined to carry on working to do what little I could to help them too.

Back at home my thoughts turned to Bourj al Barajneh. I missed my Palestinian friends and wondered if and when I would see them again. Would they all still be alive? Would they ever be free from danger and persecution? Would the children ever know a life without snipers and mortar bombs? Would they ever have their own homes in their own land?

I am afraid the answer is that they will not – not until more have died and more lives have been shattered. But I do believe that eventually there will be peace and justice for the Palestinians and the Lebanese. How soon depends upon the politicians. Until then health workers like myself will continue to work with the local institutions providing health care for the people.

The world may choose to forget those people and their plight, but I for one will never forget and one day I will go back.

John Pilger
Heroes £4.50

'A tough, responsible book . . Pilger's strength is his gift for finding the
image, the instant, that reveals all; he is a photographer using words
instead of a camera' SALMAN RUSHDIE, OBSERVER

'Pilger is the closest we now have to the great correspondents of the 1930s
. . . The truth in his hands is a weapon, to be picked up and brandished –
and used in the struggle against evil and injustice' GUARDIAN

'He is a true model for his peers and followers. Let them study for instance
the awesome opening pages of the long chapter, 'Year Zero', which
unforgettably describes the hideous and desolate remains of murdered
Phnom Penh . . . mark, shudder, reflect and profit. There are other passages
just as fine' SPECTATOR

'If I were a modern history teacher, I'd start the year's course by slinging
copies of it across the desk and telling them to get on with it'
DUNCAN CAMPBELL, CITY LIMITS

Charles Humana
World Human Rights Guide £4.95

This unique survey – the very first of its kind – of 120 major countries
throughout the world records human rights performance and reponses to
the Universal Declaration of Human Rights and United Nations treaties. The
information on which it is based has been drawn from world human rights
organisations, official and unofficial sources, international institutions, as
well as individuals.

The survey is in the form of forty questions and answers, covering both
traditional human rights, such as freedom of expression association and
movement, and the wider area of state power-censorship of the media,
telephone tapping, extrajudicial killings, independence of courts, the right
to practise any religion, to use contraceptive devices, to practise
homosexuality between consenting adults. The results are calculated and
summarised by an overall rating.

All Pan books are available at your local bookshop or newsagent, or can be ordered direct from the publisher. Indicate the number of copies required and fill in the form below.

Send to: **CS Department, Pan Books Ltd., P.O. Box 40, Basingstoke, Hants.   RG21 2YT.**

or phone: 0256 469551 (Ansaphone), quoting title, author and Credit Card number.

Please enclose a remittance* to the value of the cover price plus: 60p for the first book plus 30p per copy for each additional book ordered to a maximum charge of £2.40 to cover postage and packing.

*Payment may be made in sterling by UK personal cheque, postal order, sterling draft or international money order, made payable to Pan Books Ltd.

Alternatively by Barclaycard/Access:

Card No. [ ][ ][ ][ ][ ][ ][ ][ ][ ][ ][ ][ ][ ][ ][ ][ ][ ][ ]

Signature:

Applicable only in the UK and Republic of Ireland.

While every effort is made to keep prices low, it is sometimes necessary to increase prices at short notice. Pan Books reserve the right to show on covers and charge new retail prices which may differ from those advertised in the text or elsewhere.

NAME AND ADDRESS IN BLOCK LETTERS PLEASE:

....

Name————————————————————————

Address————————————————————————

————————————————————————————

————————————————————————————

————————————————————————————

3/87